PEACE

THE PEACE MISSION MOVEMENT

Founded by
REVEREND M. J. DIVINE
Better known as FATHER DIVINE

THE PEACE MISSION MOVEMENT

Founded by
REVEREND M.J. DIVINE
Better known as FATHER DIVINE

As explained by
MRS. M. J. DIVINE
Better known as MOTHER DIVINE

Imperial Press, Incorporated
Philadelphia

Prepared by

MOTHER DIVINE

For the

MONTGOMERY COUNTY FEDERATION
OF HISTORICAL SOCIETIES
PENNSYLVANIA

For inclusion in its publication of

MONTGOMERY COUNTY: THE SECOND HUNDRED YEARS

CONTENTS

SECTION TWO

Supplementary reading on specific topics concerning
the Work and Ministry of FATHER DIVINE that are
widely discussed but little understood.

PHOTOGRAPHS

FOREWORD

In the year 1884, the *History of Montgomery County* edited by Theodore W. Bean was published. This was a comprehensive, 1200 page history of Montgomery County in Pennsylvania, covering the hundred years beginning with 1784 when, on September 10, Montgomery County was established as a political entity.

The Montgomery County Federation of Historical Societies is undertaking a similar history of the second hundred years of Montgomery County, edited by Jean Toll. It is scheduled for publication in 1984.

Editor Toll has requested MOTHER DIVINE to supply for this work an account of the activities of the Peace Mission Movement which have been carried on in Montgomery County between 1884 and the present. Pertinent background information concerning the Work and Ministry of FATHER DIVINE prior to its advent in Montgomery County in 1952 has also been included.

Editor Toll supplied all the religious bodies represented in the work with identical guidelines for writing their respective accounts. The following account has endeavored to stay within these guidelines as much as possible. To a certain extent, following the outline limited the describing of the somewhat unorthodox beliefs and practices of the Peace Mission Movement. On the other hand, following the outline brought out various aspects of the Movement about which little was generally known.

The following work differs from the report submitted to the Montgomery County Federation of Historical Societies only in minor revisions and refinements, except for chapters added to Section Two. Section One contains a brief account of the Work and Ministry of FATHER DIVINE and the activities carried on by HIS Peace Mission Movement.

In preparing the manuscript for publication it was thought expedient to give coverage also to certain veiwpoints, concepts, situations, proposals and events in the ongoing of the Movement which have provoked much debate without benefit of clear comprehension of factors involved.

FOREWORD *(continued)*

These topics are presented in Section Two—for the most part in FATHER DIVINE'S own Words, or in words that HE directly and Personally inspired in others, or in MOTHER DIVINE'S own Words.

The account in Section One serves as a base from which excursions into the topics treated in Section Two may be made. After digesting Section One, the reader will easily be able to weave these topics into the fabric of the Peace Mission Movement.

There may be space in the history to be published in 1984 for only a fragment of this work. However, an unabridged copy will be filed in the County Archives in Norristown, Pennsylvania.

The vignette on the cover is a composite of Peace Mission symbols. At the top is the ascending Dove of Peace mounted in bronze on the interior wall of the Shrine to Life on the Woodmont Estate. The face of the Angel below it is taken from the wood carving between the windows of the Chapel Dining Room at the right of FATHER'S and MOTHER'S chairs. The script letter "D" calls to mind the tremendous scope of the Work and Ministry of FATHER and MOTHER DIVINE. "Rosebuds" are the young ladies who form the official choir of the Movement—FATHER always wearing a rosebud on HIS lapel. Below the Rose is the thirty-two room, French Gothic castle at Woodmont.

Beneath the castle is the Shield of Righteousness which the men's brotherhood called the "Crusaders" carry in all of their endeavors. Under the Shield is a Lily—the flower of the ladies' "Lily-Bud" group. At the bottom is the minaret-like Tower whose base is set in the exterior wall of the castle just above the cornerstone. On the sculptured cove at the top of the walls in FATHER'S Office, the motif is the leaves and fruit of the grape-vine. This motif provides a lattice-work in the vignette on the book cover that supports and is interlaced with the symbols described above—grapes signifying Victory.

The Woodmont Estate
1622 Spring Mill Road
Gladwyne, Pennsylvania 19035
April, 1981 A.D. 35 F.D.

PEACE

THE PEACE MISSION MOVEMENT

SECTION ONE

Woodmont, The Mount of the House of the LORD, Gladwyne, Pennsylvania

CHAPTER 1

Overview of the Peace Mission Movement

INTRODUCTION

THE PEACE MISSION MOVEMENT came to Montgomery County in 1952 when the followers of FATHER DIVINE purchased the Woodmont Estate, comprised of approximately seventy acres, located at 1622 Spring Mill Road in Gladwyne, Pennsylvania.

The Movement, founded by the REVEREND M. J. DIVINE, better known as FATHER DIVINE, at this time was well established in Philadelphia. There was the Circle Mission Church, Home, and Training School of Pennsylvania, 764-772 South Broad Street in South Philadelphia, the Unity Mission Church, Home, and Training School, 907 North Forty-first Street in West Philadelphia, and the Nazareth Mission Church and Home, 1600-1614 West Oxford Street in North Philadelphia. These were the churches at which religious services were held and which housed the members of the congregation on a donation-for-services-rendered basis, and offered low-cost meals to the public, as well as the services of a barber shop and dress shop.

Then there were the hotels in Philadelphia that offered accommodations, at rates comparable to the YMCA, to those of the general public who were willing to comply with the moral code of the Peace Mission Movement. These were the three-hundred-room Divine Lorraine Hotel at Broad Street and Fairmount Avenue, seven blocks north of City Hall, and the Divine Tracy Hotel near the University of Pennsylvania campus at Thirty-sixth and Chestnut Streets.

There were twelve sorority and fraternity homes and numerous small businesses.

The assessed valuation of the Philadelphia properties on which taxes were paid in 1957 was $885,000.

FATHER DIVINE moved HIS residence from New York City to Philadelphia in July of 1942 after an official delegation, headed by Judge Harry S. McDevitt, came to New York especially to extend to FATHER DIVINE the invitation to come Personally to the City of Brotherly Love and establish HIS Work and Mission there.

The powerful influence of FATHER DIVINE had been very evident world-wide and especially in New York State for a decade. HE became well-known to the public in 1931 while HE was carrying on HIS Work and Mission in Sayville, Long Island, New York. The influx of people into this small, quiet, fishing village alarmed and disturbed the townspeople. After their hostility precipitated a court case, FATHER DIVINE chose to move HIS residence to New York City, where HE could minister to the physical and spiritual needs of the masses that called upon HIM.

FATHER DIVINE changed the thinking and living of large numbers of people, so as to cultivate the climate of peace and goodwill between the races, make them industrious, independent, tax-paying citizens instead of consumers of tax dollars on the welfare rolls, and most stressfully to turn them from the selfishness, graft and greed of existentialism and the ruthless ideology of Socialism and Communism to the ideology of responsible, ardent patriots of America.

The appeal of FATHER DIVINE that initiated the Peace Mission Movement as an organization in the early thirties (see affidavits of John Lamb, Charles Calloway, Captain Millard J. Bloomer, John Henry Titus and Eugene Del Mar in Chapter 7) was as follows:

1. The love and benevolence of FATHER DIVINE supernaturally extended to whomever came within its radius;

REVEREND M. J. DIVINE

19

2. The revelation to countless numbers that the long-awaited Second Coming of JESUS CHRIST was here and now in their time in the Person of FATHER DIVINE;

3. The simple living of the Teaching of JESUS CHRIST in all sincerity that automatically made Christianity practical and workable to solve individual, social, national and international problems.

This is what converted the masses to follow FATHER DIVINE.

BECOMING A FOLLOWER

A person does not become a follower by "joining" the Peace Mission Movement in the manner that a person joins an orthodox church. The person first comes in contact with the Name of FATHER DIVINE in some way. Because the person is thus harmonious to the Truth, he or she is encouraged to incorporate as much as possible of FATHER DIVINE'S Teachings into his or her own everyday life and affairs. According to the sincerity and conscientiousness of the individual, he or she grows into being a follower and unfolds from one degree to another. A person is a follower to the degree that he or she follows the Life and Teachings of CHRIST according to FATHER DIVINE'S Conviction and becomes a living epistle seen and read by men.

DESCRIPTION OF A FOLLOWER

Followers of FATHER DIVINE have these distinguishing characteristics:

1. They are real Americans in that they are people of different racial, national, religious and social backgrounds.

2. They believe in the Brotherhood of Man under the Fatherhood of GOD and never use terms that separate or designate one from another in a discriminating way.

3. They live celibate lives and do not associate with the opposite sex except when necessary for conducting business.

4. They are industrious, thrifty and honest, giving an honest day's work for an honest day's pay.

5. They are completely independent and self-supporting in every way.

6. They will not beg, borrow or steal.

7. They will not accept gifts, tips or bribes, vacation pay, social security benefits, insurance benefits or legacies or anything they have not earned or paid for.

8. They pay all their debts and pay cash for all purchases and buy nothing on credit or the installment plan.

9. They do not smoke, express vulgarity, profanity or obscenity.

10. They do not imbibe intoxicating liquors or drugs.

11. They do not gamble, wager or patronize lotteries.

12. They do not insure their lives, the lives of others or their possessions.

13. They are happy, peace loving and work for brotherhood and unity and are opposed to fighting, war and violence of all kinds.

CHAPTER 2

Structure of the Peace Mission Movement

ECONOMIC FOUNDATION

UPON BECOMING A FOLLOWER OF FATHER DIVINE, one immediately takes steps to do the following:

1. Right any wrongs one did in the past.
2. Pay all one's indebtedness, start paying as one goes, and be self-supporting.
3. Take care of all one's responsibilities in providing for any children one might have until they are sixteen or until they graduate from high school.
4. Refrain from using monies for any sort of gambling, smoking, drinking, drugs, unevangelical entertainment or using cosmetics excessively.

After taking these steps, it is not long until the individuals are able to save money, and as it is against their religious conviction to invest in stocks and bonds and also against their religious conviction to hoard money, they contribute, if they wish, to the Peace Mission Cooperative System that purchases property to be used for the advancement of FATHER DIVINE'S Work and Mission, thereby putting the money to exchange for the common good of humanity. This is done absolutely volitionally with no soliciting or coercion.

Followers desire to do unto others as has been done unto them by FATHER DIVINE. They do not seek honor and glory but want to see others blessed even as they have been. They know FATHER DIVINE'S Name, not theirs, is a blessing to the people. Therefore they adhere strictly to the admonition of Jesus in the Sermon on the Mount. Matthew 6:1, 3

> "Take heed that ye do not your alms before men, to be seen of them: otherwise ye have no reward of your Father which is in heaven. . . .
>
> "But when thou doest alms, let not thy left hand know what thy right hand doeth."

The followers own the properties. FATHER DIVINE dedicated them to magnify the Law of Americanism, Brotherhood, Christianity and true Judaism as synonymous. Because the followers truly wish FATHER and MOTHER DIVINE to be praised and honored, the properties are operated under Their Spiritual Guidance and it appears as though the properties belong to THEM Personally, but the followers are the legal owners. A group of followers holds title to the property with right of survivorship, but if and when it is sold, as many properties have been, the living owners share equally the amount received from the sale. FATHER and MOTHER DIVINE own no properties or securities of any kind. The followers pay real estate and other taxes as levied. The owners have not sought tax exemption on privately owned properties. Properties owned by the Churches and operated solely in the service of the Church and the community are tax exempt.

COMMUNAL LIVING

The members or followers live in the Churches or Extensions of the Churches, such as sorority or fraternity homes. Brothers and sisters are accommodated in separate buildings or on separate floors, and this applies to husbands and wives coming under the jurisdiction of the Peace Mission Movement. Children brought by their parents live with other children under the care of guardians. When they come to responsible age, they make their own decision to remain in the Peace Mission or leave.

There is complete integration. No attention is paid to the so-called race, creed, color or national origin, except to have individuals of different complexions eat, sleep and live together as roommates.

All residents of a Church or building under the jurisdiction of the Church adhere to FATHER DIVINE'S International Modest Code, which is,

" No smoking, no drinking, no obscenity, no vulgarity, no profanity, no undue mixing of sexes and no receiving of gifts, presents, tips or bribes."

For further explanation of standard Peace Mission policy, see FATHER DIVINE'S letter in Chapter 6.

Followers may work at whatever labor, trade, or profession they choose, and they may do whatever they wish with what they earn or possess. However, they donate for living accommodations, meals, and other services such as laundry, dress-making, tailoring, barber service and transportation.

CO-WORKERS

The privileged ones who operate and maintain all Church properties and Church business and affairs are called co-workers, because they are working together with FATHER and MOTHER DIVINE for the benefit of mankind generally. Neither they nor FATHER and MOTHER receive a salary or remuneration; they give their services gratis because they love GOD and humanity. All of their needs, comforts and conveniences are bountifully supplied by the Church or business.

Followers who have fallen prey to old age and have been true and faithful co-workers are taken care of by the Church as long as possible. The Church does have homes for the aged, but no hospital or convalescent-nursing home, there purposefully being no systematic or practical preparation for old age. The true followers are content with their conviction that "The just shall live by faith," Galatians 3:11 and "He who puts his trust in GOD shall never be confounded."

CHURCHES OF THE PEACE MISSION MOVEMENT

The Peace Mission Movement itself is not incorporated, but the Churches under it are. In the year 1981 there are the following organized Churches incorporated in various states and countries with branches:

The Circle Mission Church, Home and Training School, Incorporated

The Nazareth Mission Church and Home, Incorporated

The Unity Mission Church, Home and Training School, Incorporated

The Peace Center Church and Home, Incorporated

The Palace Mission, Incorporated

These Mother Churches were all incorporated in New York in February, 1941, except for the Palace Mission which was incorporated there on March 19, 1940. In foreign countries as in other states of the United States, people in different localities have embraced the Teaching of FATHER DIVINE and desired to unite and form a Church. This has taken place specifically in Australia, Austria, Canada, Germany, Guyana, Nigeria, Panama and Switzerland. Each Church has a President, Vice-President, Secretary, Treasurer and Board of Trustees, but the Spiritual Head of the Church is FATHER and MOTHER DIVINE. No Church is bound or obligated financially to the headquarters but all the Churches have a common Constitution and By-laws.

No one is ever asked to become a member of any of the Churches; it is a purely voluntary action. There are never membership drives—and no proselyting of any kind. It is not necessary to join a Church to be a follower. No membership rolls are kept;

names are recorded only when necessary for business purposes. There are no membership dues.

The Churches are founded on the Old and New Testaments of the King James' version of the Christian Bible, particularly the Life and Teaching of JESUS CHRIST as recorded in Matthew, Mark, Luke and John, and more especially in the Sermon on the Mount, found in Chapters five, six and seven of Matthew. The growth of the Church is dependent upon the Holy Spirit and also upon the living, by the members, of the exact Life and Teaching of JESUS CHRIST which when Personified in any individual or group of individuals is magnetic and will automatically draw new members into the fold.

CHURCH SERVICES

Church services are held in the Church auditoriums every Sunday throughout the year and also on as many evenings during the week as possible or convenient. They consist of public singing of inspirational hymns and songs as the Spirit moves, scriptural reading from the King James' version of the Holy Bible, reading of FATHER DIVINE'S Words of Spirit and Life, playing of tape recordings from the Audio Library of FATHER DIVINE'S Sermons, MOTHER DIVINE'S Addresses, and Church Services from foreign countries, sermons by visiting ministers, lectures by other speakers, and volitional testimonies from the congregation.

The services are conducted as in a great Spiritual Democracy, which is what the Churches of the Peace Mission Movement really are. The privilege of free speech and volitional expression is preserved for everyone. Each and every individual can speak according to the dictates of his own conscience as long as he does not infringe on or abridge the rights of others. No collections, donations or love offerings are taken up at Church Services.

HOLY COMMUNION SERVICES

Holy Communion is the only Sacrament observed by the followers and is performed daily as a ritual in the Churches and

27

private homes. Followers believe that every Holy Communion is served by FATHER and MOTHER DIVINE, whether Personally or Impersonally, and the Presence of FATHER and MOTHER is always in evidence in the brotherhood, joy and abundance of these Services. Followers believe in the serving of Communion daily after the manner of the LORD'S Supper, for they believe in the practicality of their spiritual devotion and service unto GOD and unto man, and the variety of food which is served for the sustenance of the body and the satisfying of every appetite is deemed to be sacred and consecrated to and for the development and improvement of the soul.

In the history of the early Christian Church, it is recorded that Communion was served every day and that Paul appointed deacons to assist with the serving. These Communion services were happy and joyous events in the manner of a love feast or fraternal meal, where everyone rejoiced in the Presence of the LORD. Followers believe that when they receive daily Communion with thanksgiving, they take on more of the spiritual nature and characteristics of the CHRIST. By so doing, they put off the old man with the Adamic state of consciousness, and arise daily and walk in the newness of life. JESUS CHRIST, our Elder Brother, fed the four and five thousand as they had need, and spiritually taught them at the same time; and there is record of His serving the Last Supper to His Disciples, which must have been only one of many. Therefore, followers of FATHER DIVINE endeavor to do likewise.

Members of other faiths and denominations, by respecting FATHER DIVINE'S Teaching, may participate in Holy Communion Services if they wish to do so. Though they may not participate wholeheartedly in the convictions of the followers, they may benefit greatly from the beauty and inspiration of the occasion. It was at the Holy Communion Table, during the years of HIS Personal Ministry, that FATHER delivered most of HIS Wonderful Sermons, through being inspired during the Service. HE never spoke from a prepared text.

COMMUNITY SERVICES

The Peace Mission has always served the community through its hotels, cafeterias, food markets, dress shops, barber shops, gas stations, shoe repairing and dry cleaning establishments and such services that provide the necessities of life at lower prices than can be found elsewhere. This is "preaching the gospel in dollars and cents" as FATHER DIVINE would say, by giving the best for the least. Therefore, HE considered these business places to be more sacred than the churches. As an Iranian student staying at the Divine Tracy Hotel expressed it,

> "This Mission is giving. It is giving in a way that the people who receive it do not know they are receiving—they would be ashamed [if] they knew what they are actually receiving. . . . This is the meaning of the work of GOD."
>
> THE NEW DAY, December 29, 1979, p. 15

Prime testimony to this concern for the people are the two hotels in Philadelphia as well as the two in New Jersey. These hotels are open to the general public—those who are willing to abide by the rules of conduct, speech and dress which the hotels maintain. These rules are most confining, but are welcomed by those who seek peaceful and quiet resting places and value the Principles of the Peace Mission. Here the ordinary man or woman can find excellent accommodations at costs that are always well below prevailing rates at other hotels.

Hotel guests come from all over the world and for various reasons. They are mainly made up of:

1. Post-graduate students, foreign and domestic, attending local schools and universities.
2. Church groups and other touring groups that come to the city for conventions.

29

3. Relatives of out-of-town patients being treated at Philadelphia's distinguished medical facilities.
4. People seeking refuge from the pressures of oppressive circumstances.
5. People who want to avail themselves of the economic advantages, in order to better their lot in life later on.
6. Career ladies and gentlemen.
7. People seeking a haven as pilgrims to a large city.

Knowledge of FATHER DIVINE had already spread nationally and internationally before the hotels were opened. As guests at these hotels come and go over the years, the benevolence of FATHER DIVINE, reincarnated in HIS followers and extended in a practical way through the Divine chain of hotels, is spread further, and is attested by the many who have returned to give thanks and say that had it not been for the blessing of eating and sleeping under the jurisdiction of the Peace Mission, they would not be enjoying their present success and prosperity.

FATHER DIVINE has always enjoyed serving Holy Communion as an abundant meal for the benefit of the body as well as food for the spirit and mind, and the public are welcome to partake of it along with HIS followers. Over the years untold thousands have come to observe the Peace Mission by this means, and large groups of students from universities, colleges and high schools have learned of FATHER DIVINE in this way. Thousands of students have come from Temple University, the University of Pennsylvania, Trenton State Teachers' College, the Union Theological Seminary, the University of Delaware, Beaver and Swarthmore Colleges, Friends Work Camps and Burlington Junior High School, to name those who have made regular visits with their professors, as part of their sociology or religious courses.

Peace Mission Churches have been active in encouraging the children of the neighborhood to do well in school by providing after-school classes and sometimes individual tutoring. At the Unity Mission Church in West Philadelphia the young people, specifically teen-age boys, have benefited by the use of the gymnasium, given freely without monetary consideration of any kind, so that they could enjoy their leisure time. The Peace Mission has cooperated with the Police Athletic League (PAL) in providing a recreational program that supported boys who did not want to be members of gangs, or had formerly been members. Together with the American Youth Academy and Camp Wingfoot, their use of the Church gymnasium and auditorium has been without any obligation, financial or otherwise.

The sincere intent of the followers of FATHER DIVINE, through the Church activities, is to develop the youth into strong, honest, American citizens. If, through their harmonious contact and participation in Church activities they become followers, it is absolutely of their own volunteer volition.

EDUCATION

The Churches and connections, having facilities for group living, automatically provide education in a practical way. This is the main provision for imbibing FATHER DIVINE'S Teaching. It is in reality a university for learning the highest unfoldment of Truth ever presented to man.

Children and adults attend schools of the community in which they live, to obtain high school diplomas. Everyone is encouraged to be schooled sufficiently to be efficient and practical in their chosen field. The Peace Mission Free Schools provide classes within the Churches also, for study of the Bible and other subjects for which there may be demand and for which there may be instructors desiring to impart their knowledge to others without remuneration.

GROUPS WITHIN THE MOVEMENT

1. Rosebuds are the feminine youth group who pattern their lives after the Virginity of Mary and the Holiness of Jesus. They are the official choir and sing during Church services. Their songs are mostly those inspired by FATHER DIVINE'S Words, HIS Work and Mission. They volitionally sing of their sacred love for GOD, their Husband and Maker, as well as of their love for America, Democracy and Brotherhood. Their uniform consists of a red jacket with a white "V" for Virtue and Victory, a blue skirt and white blouse.

2. Crusaders are the brothers who likewise model their lives upon the Virginity of Mary and the Holiness of Jesus, and who have totally embraced FATHER DIVINE'S Teaching. They give their time and service in the Church work and activities. They wear a light blue jacket trimmed in black with a symbolic emblem on the breast pocket, and black trousers. They wear a white jacket when they serve as waiters during Holy Communion Services.

3. Lily-buds are those sisters who were redeemed from the mortal, carnal life, and made virtuous as the Rosebuds, through living the CHRIST Life according to the Holiness of Jesus and the Virginity of Mary. Their uniform is a green jacket with the letters "H" "V" meaning Holiness and Virtue, green skirt and white blouse.

All three groups have their own distinctive Creed which each member memorizes. These Creeds set the goals of the group and outline in detail how each member should live. There is a fourth, the Woodmont Creed, which more or less epitomizes the other three as well as the relationship of all the followers to Woodmont.

PUBLICATION

A group of followers of FATHER DIVINE publish a commercial bi-weekly tabloid entitled *The New Day*. This newspaper features the work of FATHER DIVINE. From its inception in 1937, FATHER DIVINE has contributed gratis HIS Lectures, Sermons, Interviews, Letters of Correspondence and Informal Talks, as well as those of MOTHER DIVINE. The paper also contains reports of activities of the Peace Mission Movement here and abroad, local and national news, occasional feature articles, and advertisements. Further information may be obtained from The New Day Publishing Company, 1600 West Oxford Street, Philadelphia, Pennsylvania 19121. Information concerning the publication known as *The Spoken Word* may also be procured from this source.

FATHER DIVINE'S mission has always been service to the people, and to this end HE dedicated HIS Ministry. That HE succeeded is attested by action of the Council of the City of Philadelphia on February 4, 1982 A.D. 36 F.D., when it unanimously passed a historic Resolution honoring FATHER DIVINE and the Peace Mission Movement for more than fifty years of service to GOD and the community. The Resolution and a photograph of the presentation may be found in Chapter 15.

CHAPTER 3

Major Beliefs, Theology and Practices

AMERICANISM

FOLLOWERS BELIEVE THAT AMERICA, as the amalgamation of all nations, was predestined to be the birthplace of the Kingdom of GOD on earth. They consider the official documents of the United States of America—the Declaration of Independence and the Constitution with its Bill of Rights and Amendments—were divinely inspired, and that they take their places with the Old and New Testaments of the Holy Bible as instruments of the synonymous teachings of Democracy, Brotherhood, Americanism, Christianity and true Judaism. Therefore they are patriotic, law-abiding citizens. FATHER DIVINE has said,

> "The system of rising in opposition to government and to organizations and to different groups and the like—that is not according to MY Principle; but it is the amalgamation of all religions and the amalgamation of all organizations by scientifically working cooperatively and working in unison."

Furthermore, followers believe that the flag of the United States of America shall fly in every land, as the universal symbol of Liberty, Unity, Freedom, Equity and Justice, through the eventual acceptance of the Constitution of the United States by all nations.

By HIS Personal Life of Independence and Brotherhood, FATHER DIVINE set the Standard for a real American as being a citizen of the world, without being limited to family, race, nationality or religion. Therefore even in the early thirties HE

35

spoke out against the persecution of the Jews in Germany as HE did against the harsh treatment of the Scottsboro Boys in Alabama.

FATHER DIVINE maintained HIS freedom of thought and action by repeatedly refusing all financial aid, including grants from both the Ford and Rockefeller Foundations and private donations, in one instance for as much as $700,000. HE maintained HIS integrity and stood unwaveringly for HIS religious and political convictions and could not be influenced by power or money. FATHER DIVINE was exceptionally adamant in HIS refusal to depend on money in any way. See the five affidavits in Chapter 7—especially that of John Lamb, in which FATHER'S own Words on the subject are quoted.

At the same time, HE was feeding sometimes as many as 3,000 unemployed daily without charge, and running a free employment agency to help them find work, HIS goal being to produce a happy, independent citizenry with an understanding of their Constitutional rights and a willingness to help make laws in accord with same. HIS very Presence was an impelling moral force, which caused untold thousands to willingly forsake violence and crime as a way of life, throw away their weapons and to cooperate constructively for the advancement of others as well as themselves.

From the minds of this nucleus of people believing that FATHER DIVINE had ushered in a new dispensation for humanity, a platform for righteous government was drawn up in 1936, and sent to officials of city, state and federal Government, as well as to Heads of Government around the world. This "Righteous Government Platform" called for the enactment of legislation in the following specific areas:

MISCELLANEOUS LEGISLATION

1. Repeal all laws passed contrary to the spirit and meaning of the United States Constitution and its Amendments.

2. Make it a crime to discriminate on account of race, creed or color in any public place; for landlords to refuse tenants, or for employers to discharge workers for this reason; also to discriminate in hiring practices or withhold any classification of work from qualified civil servants. Segregation in neighborhoods, schools and colleges, churches, theaters, public conveyances, etcetera, to be abolished.

3. Cause nations and individuals to destroy all firearms and instruments of war saving those used for law enforcement.

4. Make it a crime for publications to use segregated or derogatory terms or write abusively concerning anyone.

5. Repeal all laws providing for compulsory insurance.

6. Abolish capital punishment in all states and countries.

7. Enact legislation to make the medical profession responsible for health and life of patient when medical treatment is mandatory. The law must work both ways.

8. Abolish lynching and outlaw members of lynch mobs in all states and countries.

9. Immediately return to owners all goods and lands stolen by individuals and nations.

10. Establish a maximum fee for all labor union membership, causing them to accept all qualified applicants and give them equal privileges regardless of race, creed, color or classification; also to provide that any labor union which limits the hours and days of work per week, must guarantee at least that much work per week to its members, and if it calls a strike, pay its members while they are out of work, the full amount they are demanding from the employers; otherwise all obligations for dues must cease.

11. Repeal legislation requiring individuals to designate themselves as being of race, creed or color in signing documents.

ECONOMIC LEGISLATION

1. Authorize employment agencies to collect fees from employers and prohibit collection of remuneration from employees or sending them out for less than minimum wage.

2. Authorize Government control of all idle plants and machinery, tools and equipment, where owners are unwilling to operate them at full capacity; such facilities to be made available to workers on a cooperative, non-profit basis under supervision of Government experts; workers to be paid a living wage until income exceeds expenses, then the wage scale to be increased and maintained at as high a rate as conditions permit. The owners would have the privilege of operating the plants at any time they were willing and able to operate them at full capacity, or until some arrangement be made for change of ownership.

3. Abandon regulations requiring individuals to be on relief rolls to get work on relief projects.

4. Immediately provide, under Government supervision, work on useful projects for every unemployed worker according to his qualifications, with suitable pay for amount of work accomplished. Expenditures for many such projects, such as high speed tunnels, express highways, or whatsoever it might be, could quickly be regained by tolls, as in the case of the Holland Tunnel in New York City.

5. Abandon Government crop control and destruction of foodstuffs in all states and countries; equitable distribution to be established.

6. Institute free trade and abolish all the tariffs among nations.

7. Limit profit and permit individuals to sell for as little as they choose.

8. Authorize Government to print its own money and make it illegal to hoard it. Government to redeem all its bonded debts and to lend the money to the cooperative non-profit enterprises; abolish all interest and make it a criminal offense to take usury or interest, or to receive dividends that exceed 3½ percent, or money without labor performed or practical service rendered.

9. Authorize Government ownership and operation of the financial system.

10. Make it a criminal offense to spend money for other than necessities while owing a just debt.

11. Request destruction of all counterfeit money by individuals or whoever may acquire it.

POLITICAL LEGISLATION

1. Provide for nomination by the people of all candidates, including those for President and require them to meet specified standards to prove their qualifications for office, not as politicians but technical experts.

2. Appoint all civil servants according to qualifications without discrimination, patronage or intervention of political leaders.

EDUCATIONAL LEGISLATION

1. Provide universal education with same rights for all, including technical and professional training.

2. Abolish in all educational institutions and from books used for educational purposes all references to racial conflicts or differences, national glory through military feats, etcetera, with legislation making it a misdemeanor for any educator to teach such to his classes.

3. Abolish the greeting "H-e-l-l-o" in educational establishments by substituting the word "Peace." Cooperation of
   telephone companies requested in this respect.
4. Adopt a universal language for all nations, languages,
   tongues and people.

The full text of the Righteous Government Platform can be found
in Chapter 14.

FATHER DIVINE has always endorsed the public school system
and encouraged people to qualify themselves that they might work
according to their calling and develop their capabilities. Around
five thousand of HIS followers returned to school at this time.
They were working during the day and putting their savings into
real estate at the advice of FATHER DIVINE, sometimes buying
homes which were operated cooperatively to establish a pattern of
integrated living in segregated neighborhoods.

Some of these properties were farms in upstate New York, for
FATHER DIVINE had also in mind to make the land more produc-
tive and plots of land were offered free to those willing to build
homes and begin cultivation.

FATHER DIVINE has always encouraged the people to be self-
supporting and independent. It was estimated that during the years
of HIS Ministry in New York, the city was saved three million
dollars annually by HIS followers coming off the relief rolls, and
the crime rate dropped in areas of HIS activities.

Followers of FATHER DIVINE, under HIS instruction, paid the
cost of citizenship papers for aliens who desired to become first
class citizens.

As the prospect of World War II drew closer, the Palace
Mission Church in New York offered accommodation for hospital-
ization in case of an emergency and brothers and sisters
volunteered as air raid wardens and first-aid personnel. There was
no evasion of the draft when it was instituted; some followers

enlisted; others, with the religious conviction not to fight for any cause, suffered imprisonment or went to work camps.

Meanwhile, on September 20, 1938 before hostilities commenced, FATHER DIVINE had suggested to the Heads of the American Government and of other countries concerned, that the disputed Czechoslovakian territory be purchased, as a practical way to pray for and attain Peace before rather than after war. When the war did break out in Europe, HE suggested that the Three Americas be united as a national and international defense for Peace. In this unification there would be ample national and natural resources, as well as manpower, to ward off any invasion of the Western Hemisphere. This proposal on December 9, 1939, went unheeded, and when the United States became involved in war, in order to give every possible assistance to the Allies, that Democracy might win the battle against Fascism and Nazism, the followers bought millions of dollars worth of United States Bonds, in most cases making the Government the beneficiary. (Proposal made January 12, 1944.)

To provide much needed accommodation for the Coast Guard stationed on Brigantine Island near Atlantic City, the beautiful Hotel Brigantine on the ocean front, owned by the followers, was given gratis in 1942 for the use of the Coast Guard for the duration of the war, the only stipulation being that there be no segregation. The Coast Guard was already integrated; whereas the Armed Forces were not integrated until July 26, 1948.

FATHER DIVINE continued HIS proposals and declarations for Peace as follows:

July 6, 1944. Proposed the unification of all mutual and allied sovereignties of the universe that the united countries of the world be one big universal allied sovereignty.

May 7, 1945. Sent a letter to Premier Hirohito, demanding Japanese unconditional surrender or take consequences of being annihilated.

October 23, 1945. Urged re-conversion and reconstruction for universal Peace and tranquility, recommended unity and mass production to win the victory in Peace as it had been won in war.

July 1, 1946. Recommended an extension of price control.

December 9, 1946. Proposed that the United Nations accept Philadelphia as the capital of the United Countries of the world.

June 11, 1947. Appealed to Federal Government to cross borders of sovereign states and break laws that are unconstitutional and endorse segregation.

April 29, 1948. Declared an international holiday commemorating the Marriage of CHRIST to the Church, to bring about the Universal Brotherhood of Man and the propagation of Virtue, Honesty and Truth.

August 6, 1948. Declared that this is GOD'S Administration and that this whole civilization shall have a new birth of freedom.

April 25, 1949. Declared all nations shall be guided by the Pendulum of Equilibrium. The unification of all nations, or Allied nations is the only hope of the salvation of any nation.

March 14, 1950. Declared HE had broken the line of demarcation between all nations, thus advancing the cause of Civil Rights; but it was being shown only gradually in different demonstrations of the present, such as the African Prince's marriage to the English schoolgirl.

March 16, 1950. Supported President Truman's decision to build the hydrogen bomb.

May 6, 1950. Proposed that Australia and New Zealand accept United States Constitution and unify with America.

July 28, 1951. Proposed retroactive compensation for African slaves and their descendants, and other underprivileged subjects.

September 14, 1951. Advised acceptance of Chiang Kai-Shek's
Government of Nationalist China, granting them full status
with other Allied nations.

The full text of all these peace proposals, including a letter to
Japan's Premier Hirohito requesting and demanding Japan to
surrender, can be found in Chapter 13.

FATHER DIVINE continued HIS relentless crusade for the
unification of men and nations by making known to officials of
city, state and federal government within the United States and
abroad, HIS proposals that would bring Peace and prosperity.
Many of these proposals were published in the form of stickers
that were sent out on all of HIS correspondence, and were
available for similar use to all who were one with FATHER in HIS
great Plan and Purpose.

Americanism, to the followers of FATHER DIVINE, is Christianity translated into Government and called Democracy, and HE
has said,

*"In the defense of Democracy I stand, recreating a civilization
that will live the precepts of the Teaching of Jesus in deeds and
actions. Herein lies the strength of Americanism!"*

Because of this, the Churches which bear the Name of FATHER
DIVINE in all parts of the world, fly the American Flag with their
national flag. Whatever country they are in, they consider
themselves Americans and live according to the Constitution of
the United States.

FATHER DIVINE states,

*"The American Ideal of Democracy, of Freedom, Equity,
Humanity and Justice for all men, both at home and abroad, is a
vision that I must fulfill, for America has pledged her faith in the
Omnipotent One and placed her land under the guidance and
protection of the Almighty."*

CONCEPT OF GOD

In selecting, electing and enthroning GOD as supreme in one's life and as dwelling at the Center from which the cause and effect of one's being and existence emanate, it is with the understanding that GOD is the Creative Force of the Universe, the Universal Mind Substance, the Fundamental Principle and Source of all Goodness — Onnipotent, Omniscient, Omnilucent and Omnipresent.

One recognizes that man and woman were created by GOD and in HIS Image and Likeness enjoyed HIS Presence in complete unity and oneness. By being endowed with the Divine Right to choose, Adam and Eve chose to disobey GOD, and the curse of death thereby passed upon all men. Through losing the Consciousness of GOD'S Presence, man deteriorated into sin, debauchery, ignorance, strife, misery, sickness and woe. The Light of GOD'S Presence has since appeared to him during his long and arduous upward trek back to his Divine "roots" in whatever ways and appearances were the most appropriate to reach his conscious mentality on the plane of unfoldment where he was functioning at that time.

Through Mary's virtuous Mind concentrating vividly on GOD and magnifying HIS Majesty, She mentally and spiritually contacted GOD, and Her immaculate conception of HIM gave birth to Jesus. Jesus, in the Sonship Degree, materialized and personified the CHRIST, and through the death of self, He was resurrected by the Power of CHRIST within and ascended to His Bodily At-one-ment with GOD, where as a representative of humanity He overcame the curse of sin and death.

In that He came "in the likeness of sinful flesh, and for sin," He "condemned sin in the flesh." Romans 8:3 He is the Sample and Example, the Way, the Truth and the Life, by which all mankind can regain At-one-ment with GOD. "For as in Adam all die, even so in Christ shall all be made alive." I Corinthians 15:22 However, Jesus in the

Sonship Degree knew that He did not have the power to effect the universal emancipation of man. Therefore, He had to ascend to the FATHER and come yet again in the power of the FATHERSHIP Degree of expression for this universal resurrection and complete redemption of all mankind. According to the conviction through revelation to the followers of FATHER DIVINE, HE is that One come again.

HE came as a thief in the night. HE came in the "valley of the nations." HE came healing the sick and raising the dead; HE came feeding the hungry and clothing the naked; HE came teaching and preaching Life and that more abundantly. HE is the Way, the Truth and the Life in this present day and in this present time, and it was revealed to twenty-two millions (estimate made at the Righteous Government Convention in New York City in 1936), who were willing to leave all that their former life and way of thinking consisted of, to embrace the New Life in the Consciousness of GOD'S Presence here on earth.

FATHER DIVINE is the Person of the Impersonal. HE came in this expression for the purpose of lifting mankind out of the personal into the Impersonal. HE let everyone know it is nothing HE does as a Person to reach anyone's condition or circumstance, but if one contacts HIM mentally and spiritually one gets the desired results, and it would not matter where one was geographically, for HE is Omnipresent and Ever Present. It is according to the faith of the individual, and with or without HIS Personal Presence HE is just the same.

FATHER stressed living the Life of CHRIST and being the same in HIS Personal absence as in HIS Personal Presence. HE let HIS students and adherents know it was *not* necessary to come where HE was Personally to get a blessing or to live the Life. HE said HE was a Sample and Example for them to copy after, coming as a free gift to the world, gratis to mankind, coming as the poorest among men, yet making many rich. HE said, "My Spirit is your spirit, if you can receive it." HE admonished them to take on HIS

Nature and Characteristics and be willing to be a servant of all.

The Peace Mission Movement, through its organized and incorporated Churches, provides the proper spiritual climate and controlled environment that make it infinitely more possible for one to live the Evangelical Life of CHRIST within its influence than one would be able to do outside of its influence—although FATHER DIVINE says it is possible to do it, through bringing the body into subjection to the Consciousness of GOD'S Actual Presence.

Therefore, it is to be understood that the Peace Mission Movement is the "general assembly and church of the firstborn" in which "the spirits of just men [are] made perfect." Hebrews 12:23 Whether one lives the Teaching in an isolated part of the world in one's own home, whether one comes to Philadelphia from a foreign country to unite with other believers, or whether one believes these same Principles of Righteousness, Justice and Truth and patterns one's life after them, never having heard the Name of FATHER DIVINE or even embracing Christianity, one is a member of the "General Assembly and Church of the First Born."

FUNDAMENTAL REQUIREMENTS

The basic goals and philosophy of the Peace Mission Movement are: (a) the establishment of the Kingdom of GOD on earth and (b) the living in the reality of Heaven on earth. This is in accord with JESUS CHRIST'S teaching people to pray, "Let thy kingdom come and thy will be done on earth as it is in heaven." In order for this to come about, there are these fundamental requirements:

1. One must select, elect and enthrone GOD as supreme in one's life and affairs. This is the first of the Ten Commandments, "Thou shalt love the LORD thy God with all thine heart, and with all thy soul, and with all thy might."

   Deuteronomy 6:5

2. One must believe that Heaven is a state of consciousness that can be attained in one's personal experience here on

earth. When produced within, it is manifested without in all aspects of life. Jesus presented Heaven in His Person because of the supreme consciousness of GOD which He manifested. John the Baptist, preaching of Jesus' coming, said, "The kingdom of heaven is at hand." Matthew 3:2 Paul spoke of Jesus as being "the firstborn among many brethren." Romans 8:29

3. One must believe in the Fatherhood of GOD, the Creator and Provider, and in the Brotherhood of Man, the created, sharing in the abundance that GOD provides, where selfishness, graft and greed are nonexistent, and where giving and loving and trusting in GOD are the only means of exchange.

4. One must believe in Virginity and Chastity, for according to Jesus, "In the resurrection they neither marry, nor are given in marriage, but are as the angels of God in heaven." Matthew 22:30 In innocence and purity one can behold GOD and HIS Kingdom, because Jesus said, "Whosoever shall not receive the kingdom of God as a little child, he shall not enter therein"; Mark 10:15 and "Blessed are the pure in heart: for they shall see God." Matthew 5:8

5. One must believe that it is not inevitable for one to suffer misery, sickness and old age; neither is there any need for death to come to the body. Jesus said, "If a man keep my saying, he shall never see death." John 8:51 Also, Elihu said to Job, "If there be a messenger with him, an interpreter, one among a thousand, to shew unto man his uprightness . . . his flesh shall be fresher than a child's: he shall return to the days of his youth." Job 33:23,25

6. One must desire to make the changes in one's life that would bring about the state of consciousness indicated in the five points above. Jesus said, "If any man will come after me, let him deny himself, and take up his cross, and follow me," Matthew 16:24 and "Whosoever he be of you that forsaketh not all that he hath, he cannot be my disciple." Luke 14:33

47

To underscore the importance of the fourth and sixth requirements, attention is called to FATHER DIVINE'S International Modest Code in Chapter 6. Followers maintain that only by adherence to this Code will national and world unity be achieved.

PEACE MISSION CHURCHES ARE UNORTHODOX

The congregation of the Peace Mission Churches is comprised to a great extent of individuals who have been sincere seekers of Truth. Many were born into and came up through Catholicism, Judaism, and the sundry denominations of Protestantism. The time came when they were prompted to seek a greater unfoldment that would make the simple but profound Teachings of Jesus real and applicable in their daily lives. From orthodoxy, these individuals moved into faiths such as Christian Science, Unity, "I Am," Rosicrucianism, and the teachings of other metaphysicians of the New Thought Movement. Because FATHER DIVINE'S Philosophy and Precepts were so similar to their own, these New Thought groups naturally discussed HIS Activities, and many of these individuals were thereby attracted to the Peace Mission Movement and the wholly unorthodox Teaching of FATHER DIVINE.

The goal of the reality of Heaven on earth and the establishment of the Kingdom of GOD on earth, here and now in this day, can come about only by unity and oneness. For this cause Jesus prayed to His FATHER,

"Keep through thine own name those whom thou hast given me, that they may be one, as we are." John 17:11

Harmonization leads to unification. First, man must live in a way to create harmony within himself. This achievement will then create harmony with his fellowman, and together they must unite with GOD as Jesus did after the Resurrection, to bring Heaven and the Government of GOD on earth.

To bring this about the consciousness of GOD'S Actual Presence with the people here on earth must be made a reality under all circumstances. The Bible relates many instances of people recognizing the fact that their GOD was Present with them then and there. "Enoch walked with God: and he was not; for God took him." Genesis 5:24 Daniel was in the lions' den when he declared, "My God hath sent his angel, and hath shut the lions' mouths." Daniel 6:22 Three men, Shadrach, Meshach and Abed-nego, were bound and cast into the furnace; yet King Nebuchadnezzar declared, "Lo, I see four men loose, walking in the midst of the fire, and they have no hurt; and the form of the fourth is like the Son of God." Daniel 3:25

GOD gave HIS only begotten Son as evidence of HIS Actual Presence with HIS creation. "Behold, a virgin shall be with child, and shall bring forth a son, and they shall call his name Emmanuel, which being interpreted is, God with us." Matthew 1:23

FATHER DIVINE has said in a Message HE gave November 20, 1949:

> "That was the Commission of CHRIST in Person and in the personage of His Disciples, to convince mankind of GOD'S Actual Presence. . . . If this Commission would have been preached persistently, conscientiously and sincerely and convictionally, the nations of the earth would have been conscious of GOD'S Presence as these, MY adherents, are conscious of MY Presence." THE NEW DAY, November 26, 1949, p.11

FATHER DIVINE'S Personal coming was to create and establish the consciousness of GOD'S Actual Presence with the people.

TOOLS WITH WHICH TO REALIZE
THE PRESENCE OF GOD

The purpose of every aspect of FATHER DIVINE'S Teaching is to direct the individual toward the development of the Consciousness of GOD'S Actual Presence. The three main tools used by FATHER DIVINE are:

1. Practice of the Presence of GOD. One's separation from GOD stems from the sin of hiding oneself from HIS Presence. Acting as though one is always in GOD'S Presence and being the same will bring the consciousness of HIS Actual Presence.

2. Visualization. "As a man thinketh in his heart so is he." Man has created the negative conditions by mentally, spiritually and physically visualizing them. To reverse the condition, FATHER stresses vividly visualizing the Positive and Perfect.

3. Demonstration. In every way FATHER DIVINE placed the positive, the desirable, the pure, the Perfect, before the physical eye as well as the mind's eye of the people.

    (a) First and foremost, HE offered HIS Own Holy Body, living among the people and Personally demonstrating everything HE asked HIS following to do.

    (b) Next, HIS Spotless Virgin Bride was offered as the Sample and Example of how the people should love GOD and consecrate and dedicate their lives to HIM.

    (c) The Holy Communion Table is a dynamic demonstration and object lesson, for here in its working order is found every ingredient necessary for mankind's redemption and advancement. It is the world that man has envisaged in miniature: Father-Motherhood of GOD, Brotherhood of Man, One Family, material abundance and splendor, harmony, system, order, cleanliness, Righteousness (Right-use-ness).

    (d) The Woodmont Estate is the demonstration of GOD with HIS people. The American heritage that produced Woodmont in an age of elegance is fused with the Spiritual Law that preserves the best that man attained and makes it available for all people. Here all the world may come to witness the Scripture fulfilled and the American Dream made a reality.

CONCEPT OF DEATH

As one is absorbed into the reality of living here and now with GOD, many forms and fashions, customs, rituals and traditions pass away just because it becomes apparent that they are no longer necessary.

In the Peace Mission Movement there are no funeral services. Followers of FATHER DIVINE believe in giving flowers to the living, and when a person dies, they adhere to Jesus' admonition to "Follow me; and let the dead bury their dead." Matthew 8:22 True followers know that every expression of love and goodness made by any person is GOD expressing through that person. Therefore, they cannot be bereaved or feel the loss of any person because GOD never leaves them, and HE continues to express the love and goodness of that person in some way. This is scripturally verified in Psalms 68:5: GOD is "a father of the fatherless" and a husband to the widow.

If a follower dies in the faith, the body is taken care of in a very simple, legal, unobtrusive way. Followers believe that the body returns to the dust from whence it came and the Spirit goes back to the GOD that gave it; HE will give it another body as it pleases HIM.

A true follower who brings his body into complete subjection to the Law of the Spirit of Life that gave JESUS CHRIST the victory will not die. This goal of Perfection is something great to which to aspire, but nevertheless it is Jesus' command:

"Be ye therefore perfect, even as your Father which is in heaven is perfect." Matthew 5:48

51

CONCEPT OF BIRTH

The real birth is to be born of GOD. All humanity has been born wrong, and should have been born as Jesus was—born of the Holy Spirit. Therefore, the people must be born again as Jesus stated to Nicodemus, "Except a man be born again, he cannot see the Kingdom of God." John 3:3 Paul told the Christians at Rome how to do this:

> "I beseech you therefore, brethren, by the mercies of God, that ye present your bodies a living sacrifice, holy, acceptable unto God, which is your reasonable service.

> "And be not conformed to this world: but be ye transformed by the renewing of your mind, that ye may prove what is that good, and acceptable, and perfect, will of God." Romans 12:1-2

Everyone who is called to live the CHRIST Life is concerned with bringing the CHRIST within to fruition, and when this is birthed out and developed to Perfection, the body will not die. If there are no deaths, there need be no births. Therefore when people cease to propagate, they will cease to die.

The followers of FATHER DIVINE are concerned with recreating the Ideas and Opinions of GOD and bringing forth new beauties in the earth through the living of the perfect Life and personifying GOD'S Virtues. As Peter said, if these virtues

> "be in you, and abound, they make you that ye shall neither be barren nor unfruitful in the knowledge of our Lord Jesus Christ." II Peter 1:8

In today's world, with the problems of overpopulation, of illegitimacy, of widespread teenage pregnancies, and children being born with handicaps, deformities, diseases and addictions that are proving to be signs of a depraved humanity, followers of FATHER DIVINE are religiously convicted of the necessity of ceas ing to propagate until one has learned to perfect oneself, that one might be qualified to bring children into the world.

Self control, not contraceptives or abortion, is FATHER DIVINE'S answer to the great need for birth control.

CONCEPT OF MARRIAGE

Under the jurisdiction of the Peace Mission Movement no marriage ceremonies are performed. Anyone who embraces the Teaching automatically embraces a celibate life. Through the revelation and conviction that FATHER DIVINE is GOD, the followers become so at one with HIM that they are joined to HIM in Spirit and in Truth as though through marriage. In Ephesians 5:31-32 it is written:

> "For this cause shall a man leave his father and mother, and shall be joined unto his wife, and they two shall be one flesh.
> "This is a great mystery: but I speak concerning Christ and the church."

Hence it follows that when one exits the parental domicile to marry, one should marry GOD, even as CHRIST married the Church. Men and women marrying GOD precludes them from taking husbands and wives as mates, and therefore frees them from ties to persons and personalities. They become independent of all other people and dependent solely upon GOD to be their Soul mate and Provider. FATHER DIVINE stresses the all-importance of mating with one's Soul mate, and having the sweet intimacy of this relationship with GOD. In a Message HE gave January 30, 1936, HE describes it:

> "GOD is your soul's mate, not matter, I AM not speaking of personality; I AM not speaking of sex, nor a visible expression; I AM not speaking of masculines and feminines. I AM speaking of the Impersonal Presence, yet with or without a person the

same forever throughout all eternity. Your soul's mate should mate with your soul continually. Even though it may be lying dormant in your subconsciousness, your soul's mate should be there, resting comfortably, undisturbed, and you should be unmoved and undisturbed saving as HE moves on the altar of the heart and causes you to cooperate with HIM."

THE NEW DAY, May 11, 1977, p.1

In the face of this prohibition on marriage in the Peace Mission Movement, it has seemed exceedingly disruptive to many that FATHER DIVINE married. With characteristic fortitude, however, HE pursued the course that HE perceived to be essential for the elevation and salvation of the people, knowing that HIS action would be widely misunderstood.

Editor's Note: In the following paragraphs, MOTHER DIVINE recounts some of the details of Her Marriage to FATHER DIVINE. Lest She be thought arrogant and presumptuous because of the attributes ascribed to Her, the editor hastens to state that MOTHER DIVINE, in the fashion of all truly great people, is perhaps the most humble of all the followers of FATHER DIVINE, in that She rests completely in the knowledge of Her nothingness and GOD'S Allness. She does not ascribe these attributes to Herself on Her own Authority. All the statements made about MOTHER DIVINE in these paragraphs were made by FATHER DIVINE—Whose Supreme Authority is beyond question.

In 1946, FATHER DIVINE chose one from among HIS followers to be HIS Bride. She, in Her Spotless Virginity, was a Sample and Example for all others to emulate. In MOTHER DIVINE, FATHER found One with love and obedience sufficient to qualify Her to unify completely with HIM. Through the perfection of the life of humanity in this One, all of humanity could be partakers of this same perfection by visualizing this Perfection in Her, and by partaking of the same consciousness of GOD'S Presence in which She lives, through self-denial and consecration.

54

MRS. M. J. DIVINE
November, 1981

The Virgin Mary recognized Her LORD and bowed before HIM in Her day. MOTHER DIVINE is the same Virgin Mary, reincarnated, recognizing and bowing before Her LORD in this day and time. She appeared first in the Person of Peninnah, who married FATHER DIVINE on June 6, 1882. Peninnah, the first Mother Divine, recognized FATHER DIVINE to be the living CHRIST. Through Their Marriage, THEY propagated honesty, competence and truth in all those who were drawn to FATHER by the revelation of the Presence of GOD on earth in a bodily form. Then because HIS Personal Ministry increased so greatly, this Mother Divine desired to pass and be reborn in a more youthful body in which She could be of greater service. FATHER DIVINE did not encourage Her in that thought; yet HE suffered it to come to pass as She wished.

Thus the Spirit of the Virgin Mary, reincarnated in the first Mother Divine, was again reincarnated in a young girl who was not under FATHER DIVINE'S immediate jurisdiction, but three thousand miles away on the west coast of Canada. When "Sweet Angel" became of age, She crossed the border to Philadelphia and declared to FATHER DIVINE, "I want to marry YOU because I know YOU are GOD." In explaining this extraordinary occurrence, FATHER DIVINE said in a Sermon HE gave August 11, 1946:

> "MY Spirit went across the border and taught this virtuous, untouched, incorruptible and undefiled Bride from infancy— taught Her Americanism and the documents of our great Government until She was converted into Americanism so vividly and so conscientiously and sincerely, She desired to be an American citizen." THE NEW DAY, August 17, 1946, p.3

FATHER stated further that She could not have been worthy to marry HIM had She not been willing to sacrifice all racism and nationalism, and voluntarily leave mother, father, sisters and brothers for the gain of CHRIST Whom She loved wholeheartedly.

FATHER DIVINE'S Marriage to MOTHER DIVINE is purely spiritual. It illustrates how all others should be joined to HIM through the conviction that HE is the Personified CHRIST. Because both society and Government require marriages to be performed according to legal procedure however, FATHER and MOTHER DIVINE motored to Washington, D.C. on April 29, 1946 and were legally married.

This Marriage—the Marriage of CHRIST to HIS Church—consummated the union of GOD and man and the fusion of Heaven and earth as spoken of in the Book of Revelation. The Marriage was neither for the satisfaction of lust and passion or for physical propagation but is wholly spiritual and magnifies the qualities of Virginity, Honesty, Competence, Truth and Brotherhood. Its importance is underscored by FATHER DIVINE declaring in 1948 that April 29th be an International, Interracial, Universal Holiday.

The profound meaning of this Marriage can best be described by FATHER HIMSELF in a Sermon HE delivered on April 30, 1953:

> "As by the disobedience of one man all men became sinners and made subject to death and destruction, now as by the obedience of one and by bringing in this Virtuous, Holy, Immaculate Marriage, . . . all mankind can be purged from all dross of sin, self-indulgence, sex-indulgence, and every mortal versionated concept, that they might too, as well as those of MINE, be partakers of this innate Nature of the CHRIST that was silent in the invisible realm of men."

> THE NEW DAY, May 9, 1953, p.16

For those with eyes to see, the Scripture is now fulfilled as John spoke in Revelation 19:7-9:

> "Let us be glad and rejoice, and give honour to him: for the marriage of the Lamb is come, and his wife hath made herself ready.

"And to her was granted that she should be arrayed in fine linen, clean and white: for the fine linen is the righteousness of saints.

"And he saith unto me, Write, Blessed are they which are called unto the marriage supper of the Lamb."

THE NEW DISPENSATION

The Marriage of FATHER DIVINE consummated HIS Work of legalizing the Life of CHRIST. HIS Mind and Spirit could now go forth to universalize this Life of Honesty and Virtue as it was personified in MOTHER, practiced by HIS followers and nurtured in the Peace Mission Churches. Therefore, though FATHER'S Personal emergence on the public scene had initiated a new dispensation, designated by the addition of the letters F.D. (FATHER DIVINE) after the customary A.D. on the Gregorian (Christian) calendar, the year 1946 heralded the beginning of the new era from a calendar point of view, and is the Year One.

The emergence of a whole new technology which has made possible the exploration of space and revolutionized mankind's way of life, bringing about far reaching social changes and the emergence of the Third World nations, bears witness that since the first use of atomic energy in 1945, humanity is indeed living in a new dispensation.

CHAPTER 4

Woodmont — Fusion of Heaven and Earth

DIVINE CONCEPT OF THE WOODMONT ESTATE

IN LOWER MERION, the Palace Mission, Incorporated, of the Peace Mission Movement, owns the Woodmont Estate at 1622 Spring Mill Road opposite the Philadelphia Country Club in Gladwyne, Pennsylvania. It is private, for the use of FATHER and MOTHER DIVINE. In 1953, FATHER DIVINE dedicated and consecrated the estate as the Mount of the House of the LORD, which HE had previously described on June 24, 1953 as

> *"the repetition of history . . . as it was with the building of the Temple of the LORD in Jerusalem, in Mount Moriah, so it is in the rebuilding of the Temple of the LORD . . . at Philadelphia in Woodmont,"* THE NEW DAY, September 15, 1979, pp. 4-5

according to Biblical prophecy in Isaiah 2:2-3:

> "And it shall come to pass in the last days, that the mountain of the LORD'S house shall be established in the top of the mountains, and shall be exalted above the hills; and all nations shall flow unto it.
>
> "And many people shall go and say, Come ye, and let us go up to the mountain of the LORD, to the house of the God of Jacob; and he will teach us of his ways, and we will walk in his paths: for out of Zion shall go forth the law, and the word of the LORD from Jerusalem."

This prophecy is repeated in almost identical language in Micah 4:1-2

Woodmont was built in 1892 at an estimated cost of one million dollars by the Honorable Alan Wood, Jr., founder of the Alan Wood Steel Company of Conshohocken. William L. Price was the architect. In 1929 Woodmont was purchased by J. Hector McNeal, corporation lawyer and noted horseman, who modernized it considerably. In later years, as an ardent admirer of the Work of FATHER DIVINE, Mrs. McNeal expressed the desire that Woodmont would some day come into the possession of followers of FATHER DIVINE and in 1952, after her demise, the property was placed on sale by executors of the estate and the Palace Mission Church purchased it for $75,000 cash.

One year later, on September 10, 11, 12, 1953, after extensive restoration, Woodmont was opened to the public, and the estate—once called "one of the most magnificent estates in Pennsylvania," a symbol of the Age of Elegance when the American tycoon became her aristocracy—moved into another era, the Age of Peace and Brotherhood under the Fatherhood of GOD.

THE SHRINE TO LIFE

The Shrine to the Life, Works and Words of FATHER DIVINE was erected on an axis with the Manor House at a distance of 200 feet. FATHER DIVINE made the Supreme Sacrifice on September 10, 1965, after which time MOTHER DIVINE and officials of the combined Churches of the Peace Mission Movement collaborated with William Hyle Thompson, Architect, Richard Murphy, Associate Architect and Artist, and Donald DeLue, Sculptor, to design and construct a work befitting the Life and Ministry of FATHER DIVINE. The Shrine to Life at Woodmont was dedicated September 10, 11 and 12, 1968 A.D.F.D.

The purpose of the Shrine is twofold: providing a sanctuary in which the Body of GOD is enshrined, and acting as a reminder of

The Shrine to Life at Woodmont, Gladwyne, Pennsylvania

HIS Covenant fulfilled from the beginning of biblical history. Reminiscent of the Tabernacle containing the Ark of the Covenant, the Shrine brings the ancient and modern together. Its powerful simplicity denotes the Personal Life of FATHER DIVINE, its atmosphere of Peace conveys HIS serenity and humility, its strength and purity of line, HIS staunch stand for the high moral and spiritual values of life made clear by HIS own Example, which are the foundation stones of the Peace Mission Movement as it stands today, a bulwark of faith in a troubled world.

FATHER DIVINE'S Words on January 16, 1934 incised on the interior walls, speak of the Covenant:

> *"Condescendingly I came as an existing Spirit unembodied, until condescendingly imputing MYSELF in a Bodily Form in the likeness of men I came, that I might speak to them in their own language, coming to a country that is supposed to be the Country of the Free, where mankind has been privileged to serve GOD according to the dictates of his own conscience—coming sponsoring this Peace Mission and this spiritual revelation in the hearts of the children of men, and establishing the Kingdom of GOD in the midst of them; that they might become to be living epistles as individuals, seen and read of men, and verifying that which has long since been said:*
>
> *'The tabernacle of God is with men, and he shall dwell with them, and God Himself shall be with them, and shall be their God, and they shall be his people'."*

THE NEW DAY, February 7, 1953, p.3

It has been stated earlier that a true follower, who brings his body into complete subjection to the Law of the Spirit of Life that JESUS CHRIST taught and lived by, will not die. There is a question in the minds of many, therefore, as to the apparent contradiction of this statement by FATHER DIVINE laying His Body down on September 10, 1965, so that It could not be seen by the world.

MOTHER DIVINE reveals the beauty and profundity of FATHER'S Supreme Sacrifice on September 10, 1965, in Chapter 8.

PURPOSE OF THE WOODMONT ESTATE

Woodmont has served as a country estate where FATHER and MOTHER DIVINE and Their staff could relax. It also has served as a retreat for the consecrated co-workers from the other Churches and Connections of the Peace Mission. It is the Spiritual Center of the entire International Peace Mission Movement. Since 1953, followers have made pilgrimages to Woodmont whenever possible and as often as they can from wherever they are in the world, especially to celebrate the Anniversary of its consecration and dedication as the Mount of the House of the LORD, and the Marriage Anniversary of FATHER and MOTHER DIVINE.

OUTREACH TO THE COMMUNITY

From 1953, Woodmont has been open to the public three days annually on the Anniversary of its dedication, and in addition, since the dedication of the Shrine To Life in September, 1968, every Sunday afternoon between the hours of one and five. In the summer of 1976, Woodmont was open every afternoon for visitors to the area during the country's Bicentennial Celebration. There has never been any charge for admission nor tips or fees allowed for tours.

People come to Woodmont for many reasons, among them being:

1. To praise and worship GOD in the Highest Manifestation ever known on earth.
2. To visit the Shrine to Life to give honor and respect to FATHER DIVINE.
3. To sit down at the Table in the Chapel Dining Room as a guest of FATHER and MOTHER DIVINE and break bread

together with people of various national, racial and social backgrounds.

4. To take a guided tour of House, Shrine and Grounds and learn of the Work and Mission of FATHER DIVINE.

5. To observe the perfection of the material beauty and grandeur of Woodmont and then take it as a standard of living attainable by anyone who chooses to apply the Divine Law.

6. To contemplate and meditate in the solitude of the Shrine, along Woodmont's many winding paths and at various beauty spots.

7. To take a guided tour of a fine example of French Gothic Architecture built in America's Victorian period.

8. To study the work of William Price as a student of architecture.

9. To study the work of Donald DeLue as a student of sculpture and fine art.

10. To enjoy the greenhouses, various gardens and wooded areas of the spacious grounds in all seasons.

11. To picnic on the grounds and enjoy its recreational facilities as youngsters from the inner city.

12. To appreciate the wild life which inhabits the sanctuary afforded by the ponds and wooded areas.

CHAPTER 5

Projection Into The Future

As MONTGOMERY COUNTY moves into the Third Century and a distinctive, transcendent American Culture emerges, Woodmont will continue to actively promulgate the Moral and Spiritual Law which is the foundation of the New Culture for this New Age.

SECTION TWO

Supplementary reading on specific topics concerning the Work and Ministry of FATHER DIVINE that are widely discussed but little understood.

CHAPTER 6

Basic Policy of Conduct

FATHER DIVINE'S International Modest Code

Peace

INTERNATIONAL MODEST CODE
Established by Father Divine

NO SMOKING   ☆   NO DRINKING

NO OBSCENITY   ☆   NO VULGARITY

NO PROFANITY

NO UNDUE MIXING OF SEXES

NO RECEIVING OF GIFTS, PRESENTS

TIPS OR BRIBES

FATHER DIVINE Explains Why HIS Followers
Do Not Accept Tips and Gifts

PEACE

764-772 Broad Street
Philadelphia 46, Pennsylvania
December 20, 1945 A.D.F.D.

TO WHOM IT MAY CONCERN:

This is an open letter of information for the general public and
to those who are concerned, especially to those of the general
public, some of whom do not know why MY followers, adherents
to MY Teaching, and members of our Churches under the Peace
Mission Movement, do not take tips or receive gifts or presents of
any kind.

A true follower of MINE does not want or desire to receive a
gift or present or anything of that type for Christmas or any holiday, and considers it to be unevangelical, unconstitutional, and
not according to the Scripture otherwise; especially so long as they
are earning an independent living and expressing a real citizenry of
independence individually, even as our country declared her independence as a nation. When a person earns a salary sufficient to
meet the high cost of living and pays all of their obligations such as

may be imposed upon them, they would not and will not seek tips or presents, for the system of tip taking is trying to get something for nothing that is not justly due them.

For this cause, MY true followers, as long as they receive just compensation for their labor, business, service and trade and their merchandise, will not accept of tips, gifts or presents, for such is in violation to the teaching of the Scripture and they feel and are sure they are not living evangelical if they break any of the rules and regulations, especially when they are receiving just compensation for the service they are giving.

Many commands of GOD, laws, rules and regulations of men have been violated for the lack of understanding and for the lack of receiving just compensation for the service, labor and merchandise and personal help they are giving.

At times such has been forced upon them by panics, famines and depressions through the different political administrations which are responsible, but yet MY true followers have been for many years making good for that which they received through the depressions when they were not allowed to earn a livelihood. But since they can earn a livelihood now, they will abstain from the violations of tip taking, receiving gifts and presents, donations, love offerings or any such things that are in violation to the Declaration of Independence, for individuals should express their independence individually even as our country declared it as a nation.

The following quotations of the Scripture I add for your consideration and for the consideration of all humanity:

Exodus 23:8. And thou shalt take no gift: for the gift blindeth the wise, and perverteth the words of the righteous.

Deuteronomy 16:19. Thou shalt not wrest judgment; thou shalt not respect persons, neither take a gift: for a gift doth blind the eyes of the wise, and pervert the words of the righteous.

Proverbs 15:27. He that is greedy of gain troubleth his own house; but he that hateth gifts shall live.

Ecclesiastes 7:7. Surely oppression maketh a wise man mad; and a gift destroyeth the heart.

Isaiah 1:23. Thy princes are rebellious, and companions of thieves: every one loveth gifts, and followeth after rewards: they judge not the fatherless, neither doth the cause of the widow come unto them.

II Chronicles 19:7. Wherefore now let the fear of the LORD be upon you; take heed and do it: for there is no iniquity with the LORD our God nor respect of persons, nor taking of gifts.

Proverbs 17:23. A wicked man taketh a gift out of the bosom to pervert the ways of judgment.

Proverbs 29:4. The king by judgment establisheth the land: but he that receiveth gifts overthroweth it.

The above I wrote so that you and all may see and know the foundation upon which we are standing and why we do not want any gifts, tips or presents from any person or persons unobligated, that they and all who are concerned might be even as I AM, for this leaves ME Well, Healthy, Joyful, Peaceful, Lively, Loving, Successful, Prosperous and Happy in Spirit, Body and Mind and in every organ, muscle, sinew, joint, limb, vein and bone and even in every ATOM, fibre and cell of MY BODILY FORM.

Respectfully and Sincere, I AM

s/ REV. M. J. DIVINE
(Better known as FATHER DIVINE)

REV. MJD.p

CHAPTER 7

Witnesses of the Truth

John Henry Titus, Celebrated Poet, confers title of "DEAN of the UNIVERSE" upon FATHER DIVINE

IN AN INTERVIEW PUBLISHED IN *The Spoken Word* of September 12, 1936, John Henry Titus, celebrated poet, and author of "The Face on the Barroom Floor," states that on his recent tour of eight months through twelve states in the South he was approached by many prominent bishops, editors, professors, and persons of high social and professional standing, who questioned him as to matters and works of FATHER DIVINE. His answer to them was,

"I have the personal knowledge of FATHER DIVINE'S Work for years in New York and Eastern States, and I know that none other than one having the highest manifestation of Divinity could be accredited with such a range of expression, and such Spiritual Wisdom; hence I say HE is the Dean of the Universe.

"I have seen the transformation of lives, have seen souls lifted from the depths of degradation to be respectable, law-abiding citizens. I have known men and women changed from their impulses and passions, and elevated to heights unlike any help they could get from colleges, universities, or by cults, creeds, or isms, and given an established position, a status enviable. In all social walks, people have been lifted from lacks and despair, the weak made strong, others clothed in their right reason and settled in life. I feel I am not vaunting self in my statements, for I too, as thousands I know, have been strengthened and blessed by the personal contact of FATHER DIVINE."

Then the usual curious question was asked him, "Where does FATHER DIVINE get HIS money?" He replied as follows,

"As to your direct question concerning FATHER DIVINE, as to where HE gets HIS Money and other matters of secular interest, I will say to you as I have said in the hearing of thousands, 'What is that to thee?' By HIS Works ye shall know HIM. I have never thought about money in connection with FATHER DIVINE, for I know all things are possible with GOD. The things that interest me are: the Evangelical Life as advocated, the healing of diseased minds and bodies, the transformation of the lives of the masses, the revealing of the hidden mysteries.

"The Divine Wisdom, Knowledge and Understanding of FATHER DIVINE passes all human understanding. Were I to give you my opinion, for hours I would amplify only with eloquence, and gladness from the depths of my soul, what I know of blessings that have come to hundreds and thousands in large audiences, and communities.

"FATHER DIVINE is received and appreciated profoundly by those from higher walks of social life, and I feel the South awaking to an interest in the Spiritual Life, and a knowledge of the Divinity that it had not known before, and for this I am glad to convey my findings to you. I am happy to give you this audience on the subject of FATHER DIVINE, for I know you have come to me with hungry hearts for the truth that is stirring the world, and I feel that you are ready to receive the wonderful message that has come forth from the lips of the Dean of the Universe. I feel that you alike with others, will be ready to receive the message on hearing in a first-handed way from my lips, the Truth, and that you will give credit where credit is due. In no sense are my words intended to proselyte, but only that the Divinity I refer to in the Work and Life of FATHER DIVINE, may pervade your ministry and strengthen you in the work you are doing along constructive lines.

"I thank you for coming, for you understand and credit the words from myself unlike those of persons of casual or social life. The fact that you have come to interview me on the subject of FATHER DIVINE shows that you respect the utterance of one whom you feel you can trust to give you the Truth."

Poet Titus said in each group, he found an expression of surprise as they listened to the truth about FATHER DIVINE, and learned of HIS activities; for they had been biased by erroneous statements of press and public. However, believing the words of one whom they felt they could trust and one who spoke with authority, the earnest seekers expressed their gratitude and thanks to Poet Titus, and said they would come to New York to see FATHER DIVINE. The expression of their changed attitude reminded him of the quotation "Almost thou persuadeth me to be a Christian."

The following four affidavits were submitted to the court in the case brought by Verinda Brown in 1937 against FATHER DIVINE to retrieve money that she allegedly gave to HIM. The suit was eventually denied by the court. These affidavits, as well as the preceding testimony of John Henry Titus, are presented here in defense of FATHER DIVINE'S incomparable service to the people, which was a free gift to the world, gratis to mankind.

AFFIDAVIT OF CAPTAIN MILLARD J. BLOOMER

SUPREME COURT: New York County
VERINDA BROWN, etc., Plaintiff,
against
FATHER DIVINE, et al, Defendants
STATE OF NEW YORK,
COUNTY OF NEW YORK, SS:

CAPTAIN MILLARD J. BLOOMER, being duly sworn, deposes and says:

That I am retired, and reside at Independence Avenue and West 254th Street, Bronx, New York, where I preside over the Bloomer Estates, Incorporated. As a former resident of Harlem, a newspaper publisher for many years, and a member of Woodrow Wilson's Press Delegation accompanying him to France at the close of the World War, I was commissioned in the year 1931 to make an investigation of the Activities of FATHER DIVINE in Sayville, Long Island, for the purpose of getting facts for an exposé of His Activities.

In the Spring of 1931 I went to HIS home in Sayville, Long Island, together with a woman investigator, and remained there for a number of days. As a result of my observations during that time I was convinced that the Activities there were honest, clean and above-board, and that there were no grounds for criticism, and I wired my client to that effect.

I found a number of people living there at 72 Macon Street as guests of FATHER DIVINE, who stated that they had been homeless or destitute, and were being supported by HIM. These and the many visitors who came daily from New York City and elsewhere were entertained at large banquets that were served several times daily. I heard them testify at these feasts that FATHER DIVINE had healed them of many different diseases and afflictions, had clothed them and fed them, and would accept nothing in return for HIS Services. I heard FATHER DIVINE speak and give lectures along spiritual, scientific and Scriptural lines, in which HE said that HE had never taken up a collection, never accepted gifts or donations, and never taken anyone's money, as HIS Services were a Free Gift to mankind and HE was unobligated to anyone.

Since that time I have been in frequent touch with the Activities of FATHER DIVINE, and I have had many opportunities to test the truth of HIS statements. I myself, and many others in my presence have offered HIM sums of money to pay for hospitality and other benefits enjoyed, but HE refused to accept a penny. I have been in private conferences at Sayville and elsewhere many times, and I have never heard HIM ask anybody for a dollar nor seen HIM take one from anybody in my life.

I do know that in the political campaign of four years ago I was asked if it would be possible to get the endorsement of FATHER DIVINE for the head of the ticket, President Hoover. I told them I did not know, that it was a pretty big contract, but I would try.

I mentioned it to FATHER, and in HIS quiet way I got no reply, but about two weeks after that I received a copy of an address that FATHER had made, and some clippings from a Brooklyn newspaper in which HE had very good reason to say some very nice things about Mr. Hoover.

I knew Mr. Hoover personally, so I went down to the Campaign Committee and I told them, "You have lots of money here, and money is tight. I think it would be a nice thing to send a check for a thousand or two thousand dollars to FATHER DIVINE, because it can be put to very good use." That night I wrote a letter to FATHER DIVINE and told HIM what I had said, and thought I was throwing a little bouquet at myself, because I thought a thousand dollars might be worth while, but I got a special delivery letter from FATHER next morning and HE said, "Perhaps you do not know it, but I could not accept any money under any circumstances . . . If any check does come I will have to return it . . . As far as you are concerned you are privileged to do what you please with it." I immediatedly went down and showed that letter to the Committee, and said, "Don't put it on the books, because it is hard to get it off, and do not send any money."

Therefore no money was sent, and I received none.

Sworn to before me,	MILLARD J. BLOOMER,
this 25th day of May, 1937	Bloomer Estates, Incorporated, and
John W. Walker, Notary Public	Editor, Cooperative Newspaper
New York County	Syndicate Service, New York City

AFFIDAVIT OF CHARLES CALLOWAY

SUPREME COURT: New York County
VERINDA BROWN, etc., Plaintiff,
against
FATHER DIVINE, et al, Defendants
STATE OF NEW YORK,
COUNTY OF NEW YORK, SS:

CHARLES CALLOWAY, being duly sworn, deposes and says:

That in the fall of 1931 I became interested in FATHER DIVINE and went to HIS home at 72 Macon Street, Sayville, Long Island, where I participated in the meetings there on a number of occasions. I became deeply interested when I learned the wonderful works of FATHER DIVINE. I heard many tell of how HE had fed, clothed and sheltered them when they were destitute, and saw hundreds healed, all without money and without price.

That as time went on I became more interested and felt that I wanted to help in this Work if possible, as FATHER was the only one I had found Who was working purely for an unselfish purpose, and accepting nothing for HIS Services.

That I was independent financially, having retired from active work on the Railroads in 1927, and I offered FATHER a sum of money to be turned over to anyone HE might suggest, to help carry on this Work. This HE refused, saying that HE never solicited or accepted gifts or contributions in any form and had no connection with anyone who did, for HIS Work was absolutely independent, and HE told me to use the money for whatsoever I would desire to see HIM use it for, and HE would be satisfied.

For more than ten years I had had a number of apartments under lease on 135th Street, between 7th and 8th Avenues, in one of which at 229 West 135th Street, I made my home. In the late fall of 1931 and the winter of 1932, FATHER DIVINE was in such great demand at public meetings where HE had been invited to speak, that HE was making the trip from Sayville to New York City almost daily; and still desiring to be of service I invited HIM and HIS immediate family and guests to come and live in my home.

This invitation was accepted about March, 1932, and for about eight months my home became known as FATHER DIVINE'S New York City Headquarters, and was often referred to as the Peace Mission, a term which was rapidly growing in use among the followers.

In the late fall of 1932 I leased a house at 67 West 130th Street which was larger and more suitable for the purpose, and moved there. FATHER and a number of others who were with HIM, continued as my guests, and on account of FATHER'S Presence, my home continued to be known as FATHER DIVINE'S Peace Mission though it was merely a private home.

In the summer of 1933, one Lena Brinson, who also had a home to which she had frequently invited FATHER DIVINE, leased a building at 20 West 115th Street. This building of three stories she used for meeting rooms, restaurant, and dormitories, where she sold meals for ten and fifteen cents and sleeping accommodations at from one to two dollars per week. She came to my home several times and requested FATHER DIVINE to come and speak at some of her Meetings, and I believe HE did speak there two or three times during the following three months. She also repeatedly invited FATHER DIVINE to be her guest, and urged me on several occasions to allow her to share in the privilege of having HIM in her home Personally.

In November, 1933, after many urgent requests on her part FATHER DIVINE agreed to go, and she placed at HIS Personal disposal an office and an apartment on the top floor of the building. It was then agreed that Mrs. Calloway and I should close our home and cooperate with Mrs. Brinson in maintaining the 115th Street home, where there was room for all of us.

In this way, the 20 West 115th Street address became generally known as FATHER DIVINE'S PEACE MISSION HEADQUARTERS, and people were attracted there from all parts of the world because of FATHER'S Presence, but there is no organization, association, or organized group known as such. Those who gather there do so voluntarily; there is no list of their names and addresses, and they are absolutely unidentified. They pay no fees, make no donations, undertake no responsibilities, and there are no collections taken up at any time. FATHER DIVINE does not participate in the financing of the place, neither does HE or has HE ever received any of the returns from it. It is not connected with any other place known as FATHER DIVINE'S Peace Mission, and there is no group of individuals back of it, other than those who voluntarily devote their time and service cooperatively, in the operation of it. In fact the term FATHER DIVINE'S Peace Mission has no reference to any organized group, but refers rather to the Mission and Purpose of FATHER DIVINE on Earth, as the apostrophe 's' signifies, than anything else.

All of the other meeting places, homes, or businesses, under the term FATHER DIVINE'S Peace Mission, referred to in the affidavit of William W. Lesselbaum, Esquire, are conducted the same as those already referred to in this affidavit. They are the personal homes, or businesses, or independent cooperative enterprises of FATHER DIVINE'S followers who live and work in them. They have no connection with FATHER DIVINE Personally, although it is true, those who maintain them seek HIS Advice and Cooperation as the recognized Spiritual Head of all those who are concerned.

The 'Heavens' or 'Extension Heavens' referred to in the affidavit of William W. Lesselbaum, Esquire, do not exist as such. These must be terms coined in his own imagination or taken from the prejudicial Press. FATHER DIVINE and HIS followers stand for the one and only Kingdom of Heaven, established in the hearts, and minds, and bodies of the children of men on earth.

I know these things of my own knowledge, because as one having experience in the handling of property and business affairs, and because my home was looked upon as a sample and an example on account of FATHER'S Presence there, I was consulted by many who now operate such places, as to financial matters having to do with the operation of them.

Sworn to before me,
this 25th day of May, 1937
John W. Walker, Notary Public
New York County

CHARLES CALLOWAY

AFFIDAVIT OF JOHN LAMB

SUPREME COURT: New York County
VERINDA BROWN, etc., Plaintiff,
against
FATHER DIVINE, et al, Defendants
STATE OF NEW YORK,
COUNTY OF NEW YORK, SS:

JOHN LAMB, being duly sworn, deposes and says:

That late in the year 1930 or early in 1931, being somewhat familiar with the Works and Teachings of FATHER DIVINE, I went to Sayville, Long Island, New York, to interview HIM Personally.

That I was made welcome at the Banquet Table with many others.

That I saw the numbers of destitute persons He was feeding, clothing and housing, and I heard them testify of how they had come to HIM in sickness and poverty and HE had taken them in and healed and supported them for months and years without the cost of a penny.

That I saw hundreds of people instantly healed of so-called incurable diseases, and even blindness and deformity from birth, cancer, consumption, etcetera.

That I saw many offer FATHER DIVINE money and property in return for the blessings they had received, but HE always refused it and said HE was a Free Gift to mankind. People of wealth came, whom I personally met, and seeing the good work, they offered large sums to help carry it on, but FATHER always graciously and appreciatively declined it, saying that HE was independent of any man and did not accept contributions or donations in any form.

That I myself had in my possession at the time, more than two thousand dollars in cash, and a good deal of personal property of value. I visited FATHER one day in the early Spring of 1931 and obtained a private interview. I told HIM I desired to become a member of HIS Household and surrender all to HIM, and that I wanted to give HIM two thousand dollars that day, as I wanted it used in HIS Work.

FATHER replied that so far as the money was concerned HE could not accept it, as HE was entirely Independent and never accepted contributions, donations, or love-offerings from anyone. HE further said that it was not necessary for me to be with HIM Personally to cooperate in HIS Work, that if I wished to cooperate in such Work I could do it independently and use what means I had for such a purpose, and HIS blessing would be with me wherever I might go.

NOT NECESSARY TO CONTACT FATHER PERSONALLY

Following this I left New York on a long trip and was gone about five months. During my absence I corresponded with FATHER frequently, and I quote below excerpts from HIS letters to me:

"It is not that one must necessarily contact ME from a Personal standpoint of view to be abundantly blessed, healed and saved, but that they come to this State in Consciousness, being governed by the Spirit of the Consciousness of the Presence of GOD within themselves, for GOD is Omnipotent, Omniscient, and Omnipresent, hence a present help in every need. . . . However, if you will live exactly as stated, you are ever indeed welcome to come and partake of the Bread of Life freely here with ME, whenever you so may desire to come and visit, as your closest contact is always for your highest good."
March 27, 1931.

"And if you will abide in ME and let MY Word abide in you, living exactly according to the Life and Teachings of CHRIST as recorded by Matthew, Mark, Luke and John, you will continue to grow in Grace and in Strength and you will indeed be abundantly blessed, and a blessing to those whom you may come in contact with. . . . Not that one must necessarily contact ME from a Personal standpoint of view to be abundantly blessed, but that they come to this State in Consciousness, as GOD is Omnipotent, Omniscient and Omnipresent, hence a present help in every need. However, as long as you are lost in MY Will, you are always welcome to come Home here in America when you so may desire to do, as your closest contact is always for your highest good. For this leaves ME Well, Healthy, Joyful, Peaceful, Lively, Loving, Successful, Prosperous and Happy, in Spirit, Body and Mind." June 19, 1931.

"For it is not that one must come to ME as a Person to be abundantly Blessed, as I AM here and I AM there and I AM everywhere. But that you reach ME by Faith, from your mental and spiritual contact, and even as you were here under MY Personal Jurisdiction, so can you be wheresoever you are, as GOD is Omnipotent, Omniscient and Omnipresent, hence a present help in every need. . . . Nevertheless, if you are lost in MY Will, you are always welcome to come Home here with ME, as your closest contact is always for your highest good, that is whensoever you so may desire to come." June 2nd, 1931.

NO ORGANIZED BODY — INDIVIDUALS ACT INDEPENDENTLY

These letters were on the letterheads of Reverend M. J. DIVINE, 72 Macon Street, Sayville, New York, and they completely refute the claim of the complainant that FATHER'S Home was the

WITNESSES OF
THE TRUTH

headquarters of a cult but she was not made aware of it. These letters indicate the full extent of any organized activity. There was not then and there is not now, any organized body, group, or association incorporated or unincorporated, known as FATHER DIVINE'S Peace Mission. This term, as the apostrophe 's' implies, refers merely to the Mission and Purpose of FATHER DIVINE on earth.

All followers of FATHER DIVINE are as free as these letters indicate, to come or go without obligations, fees, dues, memberships, or even making themselves known by name. Anything they do is done independently as individuals, though they may cooperate with other individuals at times for the purpose of assisting each other as individuals, all of their activities of course being in accord with their religious conviction, and FATHER'S Teaching. If two or more get together to buy a piece of property, and one wishes to contribute the major portion of the purchase price, yet give his partners equal shares in the title, and if these partners wish to allow others who are believers in FATHER DIVINE like themselves to come and share the benefits of the property with them, it is still their individual affair; it has not become an organization nor an association.

But returning to Sayville, when I arrived there again in the fall of 1931 I stayed in the village near FATHER'S Home. While there I purchased a Ford Town Car, which I endeavored to present to FATHER, but HE would not accept it. HE told me I should use it myself, which I did.

During all this time I had been taking shorthand records of FATHER'S Addresses for my own personal use, as HE spoke at the Banquet Table daily. I transcribed these and sent copies to various friends of my own who were interested. Soon however, there was a demand for them from a number of publications, and with FATHER'S approval they were forwarded to them gratis. In this way records were made of everything FATHER spoke in public, and many things HE spoke in private, and records were also made of testimonials of followers and visitors, for the benefit of any who might find use for them.

FATHER ACCEPTED NO MONEY

Records of the testimonials of Verinda Brown may be submitted at a later date, but the time allowed to prepare an answer in this Complaint has been too short to permit reproduction of them at this time. However, to refute the charges of the complainant that FATHER DIVINE accepted money from her or anyone else for any purpose, the following excerpts are quoted from hitherto unpublished Lectures given by FATHER DIVINE in public meetings at that time. These were recorded by me in shorthand and transcribed as follows:

Delivered March 25th, 1932
72 Macon Street, Sayville

"Now someone may want to carry out another lie, and say I have asked someone for money. But that will not be a blessing to you. It will be just to the reverse. Some have come to ME who have money, and have said they wanted to help ME and such as that, and I have said, the only way I could accept anything would be for you to take this property over, if I accepted of it. . . . If you want to take this property over that is all free and clear, then I could use that means . . . or, a committee could take it over, not giving ME one penny but rather MY giving you, giving you this property for less than it is worth . . .

"I have condescended to live in this home here, and when I put the addition on to this home here, it was for the advancement of the assembly because it had advanced so that we did not have material or personal accommodation to accommodate them all. So then I put the addition on. Then it was not room, for more came—those that were poverty stricken and

86

those that were not, also. Those of you that have money, those of you that have had money, those of you that have jobs and positions and could maintain yourselves, you are here and you are welcome, so long as you are worthy, and GOD is able to supply your every need. It is Wonderful!

"Now I mentioned it some time ago to the different ones. They have come to ME and said they had money and wanted to help ME, and such as that, and I said the only way they could have the appearance of helping ME — if you want to take this property over for less than it is worth . . ."

☆　　☆　　☆

Delivered February 20th, 1932
72 Macon Street, Sayville

"The love of money is the root of all evil. Even the lack of money, the fancy for money, when it grows up it will be a love for money. I have never done a greater work than to cast out of MY own Consciousness that I have sent out on the earth plane, the love of money, for the love of money is the root of all evil. And you cannot abolish the love of money until you cast out of your consciousness the lacks, the fancies, and even the care for money. Anything that you care for and keep about, you will come to care for it."

☆　　☆　　☆

Delivered Saturday, April 2nd, 1932
72 Macon Street, Sayville

"So remember, I AM a Free Gift, and I say thou shalt not take the Name of the LORD thy GOD in vain, for the LORD will not hold him guiltless that taketh HIS Name in vain. It is Wonderful! They tried to hide from ME. They tried to take MY Name and speculate on it. I know when Billy Sunday some years ago used to come through, and when he would have a meeting he would take up a collection of thirty or forty thousand dollars, but what is thirty or forty thousand dollars in MY Sight? It is Wonderful! Listen dear ones! I would not sell MY Spirit and MY Life for thirty or forty or a hundred million dollars.

"There are others should have brought forth the CHRIST to fruition in their lives had they not allowed materialism to creep in and the love of money, speculation and graft to creep in them. They could have brought forth the CHRIST to manifestation in their lives, but they sold the Spirit, they sold it for money, and therefore they never materialized, they never developed the CHRIST. It is Wonderful! . . . Verily, verily, I say unto you, they have their reward. They have their reward when they have taken a nickel, when they have taken a dime for it. They have sold their birthright . . . I AM a Free Gift to the world, for GOD so loved the world that HE gave HIS Son. Take these thoughts in, dear ones."

Delivered August 3rd, 1932
Banquet Table, Brighton Theatre, Orange, New Jersey

"Now it will be like this all over, and everyone that will live in MY Spirit and in MY Mind and stay in this state of consciousness, they shall lack for nothing for the Mouth of the LORD hath spoken it. It is Wonderful! CHRIST, the Great Love Master in the Name called Jesus said, 'No man has left father and mother, and all of those things, houses and lands, and sacrificed all of those things, lest he don't gain an hundredfold more in this present time, and in the World to come Life Everlasting.'

"Every penny I spend rightfully and righteously, unselfishly and lovingly, with Love for MY fellowman as a free gift to them with no thoughts of return, I gain a hundred pennies for that one penny. There it is, $1.00 for every penny, and $100 for every dollar, and $10,000 for every hundred dollars, and $1,000,000 for every ten thousand dollars.

"This is the great multiplicand of Salvation brought into expression through your conscious contact with HIM that liveth forever and ever. You can do it as well as I, for GOD is no respecter of persons; neither has GOD any respect unto person or persons. It is free for you, it is free for all, and it is just as operative there as here. It is a Principle, Dear ones, free for all, and it is just the same as a broadcast message over a great, powerful broadcasting station and everyone that has a radio that is qualified, equipped, and charged, and ready to tune in on this Message that is being sent out, each one can receive it."

Delivered Friday, September 9th, 1932
New York City

"That is just a little thought as a conveyance of what one must do to receive and maintain the Infinite blessings of GOD. Now that does not say that I want you or anyone else to give ME anything. As the thought was conveyed by some that claim to be followers of MINE, some that have been out to Sayville, commonly known as the Kingdom, and stayed, and were fed and housed for many months, and coming to ME—one did—claiming that they had money and they wanted to utilize the money for MY cause, I told them the only way they could do it would be to buy that piece of property, or one of the pieces of property there in Sayville, or if they wanted ME to take anything from them to give ME a mortgage on that prop-

89

erty, as I was planning to sell, and I could not sell so readily without a mortgage, and I was planning to leave.

"Some carried out the report that they gave ME some money. Now you know you did not give ME a penny. Now the very one that talked like that was the very one, no doubt, that would not want to give anybody a penny on their tin-type. Now that one knows that they were lying. They have not given ME a penny, and have not actually offered ME a penny, but when they talk along that line, pretending to say that they gave ME money, I said, 'Now if you all, since this Movement is started and I want to sell, I will sell you this piece of property, or I will give you a mortgage on this piece of property,' or something like that. It is Wonderful!

"You see, that is the way the mortal mind always wants to carry something, and the very one that wants you to carry them. And that is why I do not take collections or any kind of foolishness like that. That is why everyone, if they want to do anything for ME I always have heretofore, and even now, I have always arranged it, I say, 'If you want to do something, I have property here, and the only way I could accept anything would be on that. . . .'

"Now candidly and frankly I can say that—not even apparently gave ME anything—because you cannot give GOD anything anyway. . . . But you have not even humanly, mortal mindedly, given ME a penny. The very one that said that, has not even apparently done it, and they talk about representing truth—representing lies. It is Wonderful! I do not even bear record of the party changing a dime for ME to call up over the telephone in a public phone booth. It is Wonderful!

"They talked about they had money and they wanted to help ME, they had been out there so long and all like that, and they wanted to help ME and so on, and I said, 'I am after selling this place and getting a mortgage on it, and that is the only way I could use your money, because the property stands for the money you see, and that is not taking anything from you. It is immaterial to ME.' And so far as that was concerned, I did sell the place. It is Wonderful! But it was not anybody giving ME anything. When they got the place, they were getting their money's worth, unless I would have sold it for more than it was worth, but that was for them to find out . . .

"That is the reason I have heretofore, up until here recently, not even allowed anyone to sweep a rug, to sweep and beat a rug on the line, unless I paid them for it. Those that were staying in the home, some stayed there for months and some stayed there for years. Now there is one that can verify that statement of his own experience. He used to go out there before he was employed in the Kingdom, for several years. He used to go out there every summer and stay in the summer, and his laundry, his meals, and everything was fixed, and he would go out and do work at his regular occupation, making five or six dollars a day, and he did not have to get a newspaper. Newspapers were bought and placed there in the home that he could read. His hair was trimmed and everything, and even sandwiches for his lunch, and did not charge for anything, did not ask for anything, not a penny. Some of them did not give even the waitresses and the cooks a pocket handkerchief, and their meals were fixed every day, and they had a chance to save four or five hundred dollars in the season. . . . 'There were ten cleansed, but where are the nine?' "

Delivered Thursday, July 14th, 1932
72 Macon Street, Sayville

"People came to Sayville; they did not know and they could not understand how these things could be. It was beyond the comprehension of the human mind. Therefore they could not, did not, know how these things could be, that GOD could set, as though a man, a table spread free for one and for all and not allow any soliciting to be done, and not allow anyone to contribute anything, and yet the abundance of the fullness of the consciousness of good, no space was vacant of the fullness thereof. They could not understand how these things could be, when I emphatically refused to allow contributions, volunteer offerings, or anything of that kind, and stood out in the Liberty wherewith CHRIST hath set you free, knowing that all good gifts and blessings come from GOD anyway."

Excerpt from a more recent Message
Given by FATHER DIVINE August 19, 1936
Published, *The Spoken Word* September 5, 1936

"We have no record of the thousands of dollars universally that are turned in daily, of lost and found money throughout the Universe, through MY Spirit of Righteousness, Truth and Justice as I have exemplified it in others through transmission and through reincarnation. We have no record of how much we are saving the welfares throughout the Universe by taking thousands and thousands and millions off of the welfares. This we have endeavored to do, even though it is detrimental to you apparently, for you at times will have to sacrifice yourselves of some limited pleasure, or blessing, or necessity apparently, for Righteousness, Truth and Justice; therefore it may work as if though a hardship upon those of MY followers to a certain degree, and would apparently work it or enact it indirectly upon ME, but for Righteousness, Truth and Justice's sake we stand and lift up this Righteous Government Platform for each and everyone to stand upon.

"Then I say, if we ourselves as individuals do not first be partakers of the fruit, others will see and know we are not endeavoring to do what we are requesting others to do, but as we endeavor to do it we are willing to sacrifice. . . . as I said years ago, if it costs ME a million dollars a day, I shall elect CHRIST JESUS as LORD of Lords and KING of Kings. I venture to say of this Righteous Government Platform and this Righteous Government Movement throughout the Universe, we are sacrificing not less than a million dollars a day for Righteousness, Truth and Justice, especially in these ways. I mean as ways, or in other words, this way of sacrificing all chances and opportunities for receiving charity through the welfares, receiving pensions and receiving insurances and other ways and means whereby we would have a right to receive. . . . we are sacrificing them, a million dollars worth a day, although I did say I would refrain from telling it."

SACRIFICES FOR RIGHTEOUSNESS

If all of the money FATHER DIVINE could have received in collections, gifts and donations had been received and accumulated by HIM, it would have amounted to many millions of dollars. If HE would ask for a dollar donation from each of HIS followers, HE would receive millions of dollars immediately. But HE has sacrificed all of this for Righteousness' sake. Is it likely then, that HE would concern HIMSELF with the few thousands Verinda Brown claims HE received from her when HE could have millions at HIS Command?

In sacrificing this and accepting not one penny, HE is the Sample of Righteousness, Truth and Justice to HIS followers, who are also learning to make similar sacrifices. They are sacrificing by not being on the relief and paying up old bills, but especially by not participating in insurances. In one recent fire they sacrificed twenty-five thousand dollars by not carrying insurance, when one of the buildings on their Ulster County properties burned down. Others are sacrificing by returning money received from insurance

93

companies in the past on account of fires, accidents, and damages to properties, etcetera. Others are constantly sacrificing by not carrying automobile insurance. In one case a $7,800 judgment was paid when less than a thousand dollars paid in insurance premiums over a number of years would have saved such a loss. Another returned about fifteen hundred dollars received for injuries under the Workmen's Compensation Law, because insurance was against his religious conviction. Others have given up their occupation rather than come under the provisions of the Social Security Act with its Unemployment Insurance and Old Age Pension features.

All of these sacrifices have been made for Righteousness, Truth and Justice's sake, and this is the Spirit of FATHER DIVINE and HIS followers. Is it likely then that either FATHER DIVINE Personally or any of HIS followers, who would sacrifice thousands and even millions without a second thought, for the sake of Righteousness, Truth and Justice, would defraud a person out of a few paltry dollars to invest in land or other scheme as the complainant alleges?

Wherefore, deponent respectfully joins in requesting that this Motion be denied, with costs.

Sworn to before me,   JOHN LAMB
this 25th day of May,1937
John W. Walker, Notary Public
New York County

Noted Author, Lecturer and Lawyer's Affidavit in Answer
to Attacks on Works and Power of FATHER DIVINE

51 Macon Street
Sayville, Long Island, New York
November 23, 1931

TO WHOM IT MAY CONCERN:

My name having been printed in the *New York Times* as a
witness in the proceedings at Sayville, Long Island, in connection
with FATHER DIVINE, I take this opportunity to give my reasons
for being at Sayville, especially as what I found here is a matter of
current public interest.

For over thirty years I have been before the public as author,
lecturer, teacher and organizer in what has been designated
variously as Mental Science, New Thought, Psychology, Spiritual
Science, etcetera; and I have been in fairly intimate association
with hundreds of other teachers who were similarly disposed. My
record will be found in most of such general books of reference as
Who's Who in America, and from time to time I have been connected with many of the best schools that have functioned or now
operate along these lines. I was attracted here to study the life and
teachings of One Whom I was advised to be a great teacher and
healer, besides being gifted with unusual powers.

In the light of this background, I have listened for a full month
to the Teachings of FATHER DIVINE. These are all given at HIS
free meals, so that eating and Teachings go together. I now
recognize in FATHER DIVINE One Whose love, charity, sympathy
and other spiritual attributes are manifested to an extreme degree
in a transparent purity of Life and to Whose wisdom and

understanding of spiritual truth I bow my head with reverence. In the words of another epoch: "I find no fault in this Man."

All that I have seen, felt and ascertained regarding the Life and Teachings of FATHER DIVINE have illumined my understanding beyond anything I have heretofore experienced. HIS Teachings are both extremely simple and deeply profound. They inculcate the practice of the CHRIST Life as recorded in Matthew, Mark, Luke and John, and seemingly HE lives this Life in its fullness. HE expounds the Teachings of Jesus as contrasted with those of Paul. This CHRIST Life HE depicts as one of extreme purity and universal Love. He cites the New Testament in support of HIS Teaching that the results of living this Life are peace of mind and health of body, together with all of the other beautiful possibilities of life. HIS Teaching is that of essential Unity and Oneness; that body, mind and soul are One; and that when the CHRIST Life is lived in its fullness, the body is spiritualized so that it partakes of the Spirit of GOD, and is no longer subject to death.

The Life so depicted certainly offers a striking contrast to the average life of humanity, and its practicality may not be understood by the vast majority of mankind. Only in the slightest degree, if any, do the Teachings of FATHER DIVINE account for the antagonism to HIM; for those who oppose HIM know little or nothing of HIS Teachings. The opposition is based on racial color prejudice, intensified by annoyance to neighbors incident to the sounds of worship, and by alleged loss of village property values. Many of HIS enemies are friendly to HIM personally, for HE expresses every admirable quality and is always kind and considerate.

In regard to HIS appearance, HE explains that it is in order that the inherent beauty of the "impersonal life" may be detected beneath an unattractive exterior. But HIS followers find in HIM equal beauty of character and countenance.

To many of HIS followers, FATHER DIVINE'S unfailing expressions and activities of love and sympathy, HIS lofty Teachings and purity of Life, and the unusual powers with which HE seems to be endowed, impel them to place HIM in a category superior to ordinary mortality, and they recognize in HIM the expected Messiah. Many address HIM as "GOD," "JESUS CHRIST," and in other terms of Divinity. But HE states frequently, that which HE does, all others can do when they think and live as HE does and have the same Consciousness.

Some of HIS familiar biblical quotations are: "I and the FATHER are One," "The FATHER is in ME and I AM in the FATHER," and "Know ye not that ye are the Temples of GOD?" Some of HIS own familiar sayings are: "GOD is here and there and everywhere," "The CHRIST in you and the CHRIST in ME will make you what you ought to be," and "The abundance of the fullness of the Consciousness of GOD—no space is vacant of the fullness thereof." A few of the frequent exclamations, "Peace FATHER," "Thank you FATHER," and "It is Wonderful."

Many have been attracted to FATHER DIVINE out of curiosity, and the fact that HE feeds freely and sumptuously from say 400 to 800 or more people each day. HE accepts no money from anyone, has no bank account, and pays cash for all purchases. HIS answer to all inquiries as to the source of HIS financial supply is: "The Spirit of the Consciousness of the Presence of GOD is the Source of all Supply, and will satisfy every good desire." Among the more intelligent and critical of HIS guests are those who claim to have actually seen HIM multiply the food before their very eyes.

Many have come here afflicted with various physical disorders and gone away healed, and some of these have returned again and again to testify to the fact. But FATHER DIVINE constantly advises that the permanence of healing is dependent upon the continued purity of Life. HE does not claim that personally HE heals anyone, or that it is necessary to contact HIM Personally for this purpose.

HE states that it is "your faith" that heals you and that you can contact HIM mentally and spiritually at any distance with the same result. Many testify that they have called upon HIS Name from a distance and have been healed — sometimes instantaneously.

Highly educated scholars have been here who have accorded to FATHER DIVINE unique and exceptional attributes; but no one has as yet solved the mystery underlying HIS Personality, wisdom, supply and power. Now that the press and radio have spread the news of HIS Activities near and far, FATHER DIVINE has become a world figure, Whose Presence and significance can no longer be ignored. It seems to be the mission and hidden purpose of all prosecutions and persecutions to bring into the light of public interest that which otherwise might remain in the twilight of comparative indifference.

s/ Eugene Del Mar

CHAPTER 8

FATHER DIVINE'S Sacrifice on September 10, 1965

Many QUESTIONS HAVE BEEN RAISED concerning FATHER DIVINE'S action in 1965, when HE laid His Body down. MOTHER DIVINE unfolds the mystery of this action in the following excerpt from an interview SHE gave to two college professors on August 26, 1971. MOTHER DIVINE speaks as follows:

". . . everyone should be glad that FATHER DIVINE came and exemplified Righteousness! HE presented Righteousness to the political world, to the educational world, the social world, the religious world—Righteousness! I mean pure Righteousness! And FATHER DIVINE stood back of that Righteousness! HE sacrificed HIMSELF for that Righteousness! HE sacrificed HIMSELF for that Righteousness and caused millions of others to sacrifice themselves for that Righteousness, and that's why that Righteousness is going to flood the earth and nothing can stop it! And that's why we're standing today!

"Without seeing FATHER as a Person, HE'S just as Real! HE said HE would never let HIS Body stand in HIS way. HE knew that HIS Personal Body was a stumbling block to many, because GOD condescended to come in the valley of the nations—come to them in a way that they would least expect GOD to come.

"Jesus came in the least way they expected Him to come; that's why the Jews couldn't accept Him. They wanted a King, but they couldn't accept Him the way He came and what He stood for. The same way with FATHER.

"He said that HE would throw off HIS Body and He would enter in, though the doors were shut! So HE'S entered in now. But HE also said, 'After I have entered in, then I will put It on again, because no man has power to take MY Life; but I lay It down and I take It up again, and I will prove to them that a Spirit has not flesh and bones!'

"But GOD is real! GOD is just as Real as you and I are Real! GOD has just as much right to have a Body as you and I have a right to have a body, because nothing is real unless it is tangible on the material plane. It is all a supposition. They have kept GOD in the spirit world long enough; they have kept HIM in the mental world; but GOD is going to be in the physical world! Isn't that wonderful? HE'S taking HIS place in the physical world now, and the kingdoms of this world will be the Kingdom of our GOD and of HIS CHRIST! . . ."

Professor: "Wonderful! Beautiful!"

WHY FATHER DIVINE CAME

MOTHER DIVINE: "When I think of the Sacrifice FATHER has made—that is why we rest, because the Sacrifice has been made, because nothing is a reality until the sacrifice is made to make it real! You know, we had the Declaration of Independence and it was just on paper, but it was because of the lives that were willing to be sacrificed to make it a reality that we have independence today.

"And that's the same way with FATHER and the Peace Mission and HIS Principles of Righteousness—not just those in the Peace Mission, but everybody, every person who is willing to suffer to establish a Principle or for a cause of Righteousness. You see, the willingness to suffer makes that particular Principle a reality. Isn't that wonderful?

"And that's why I know that with or without any of us, what FATHER stands for and what HE lives for and lived for and what

HE sacrificed for, will be! Heaven and earth could pass away, but our GOD stands firm!"

Professor: "MOTHER, YOU referred to FATHER having sacrificed HIS Physical Body. In the usual sense, HIS Physical Body d - - d. Now I understand and believe that FATHER is with us, but do YOU feel the way some religious groups feel, that HE will return again in another Physical Form? For example, the Orthodox Jews still believe that the Redeemer has not yet come. If the Redeemer is to come, well, many Christian groups feel that CHRIST is the Redeemer. Do YOU feel that FATHER will come in another Physical Form — or would YOU care to give Your views on that?"

MOTHER DIVINE: "Well first of all, I would like to say that FATHER DIVINE'S Sacrifice to ME began when GOD condescended to come in a Personal Bodily Form, when HE descended to our limited expression of life, and when HE descended to come in the appearance HE came. That was the Sacrifice. And as long as HE remained in that Body, in that limited expression so that we could comprehend HIM — this was a Sacrifice!

"FATHER DIVINE, taking on what we call the 'funeral expression,' was only another degree of that Sacrifice. It all was for the redemption of man!

"GOD, in reality, is without the beginning of days or the end of life. And GOD is not confined, and even the material world is not confined to what we see, because we see so limitedly. When we are lifted, we see a little more. Science bears record that there's sound higher than what the physical ear can hear. So you can't limit GOD, and GOD hasn't gone anywhere! HE can't go anywhere! HE IS! You understand this — GOD IS! It's just an appearance of coming and going.

"So FATHER DIVINE, GOD, chose to come as HE did for the reason HE did. HE alone knows HIS masterful Plan for the Redemption of man. We do know that FATHER DIVINE IS GOD! We do know HE demonstrated in HIS Physical Body, Youth, Vigor,

Energy unlimited! I mean unlimited! FATHER DIVINE would stay up day and night—wear out secretaries—I mean they would serve in shifts—and FATHER DIVINE would be still filled with energy and looking fresh and beautiful as ever!

"And the Power that FATHER DIVINE demonstrated! I mean, people can testify of that Power, especially when they saw people touch It inharmoniously. I mean, in those days in New York when there was so much hostility against FATHER—I mean it was demonstrated more—and like in Sayville when they were so hostile, you could actually see the electricity come out of FATHER'S Hands, and see FATHER bounce up like a ball! These are facts that many can testify to, so we know that FATHER DIVINE is just LIFE! Just LIFE!

VICTORY OVER DEATH

"FATHER DIVINE is going to fulfill the Scripture from Genesis to Revelation, and the last enemy to be conquered is death! This terrible delusion that man has been under—that he is born and he must die—but that's because he's been under that curse, under the law of sin and death. And Jesus demonstrated the Victory over it when He submitted Himself to the Will of GOD—in other words, conformed Himself to the Spirit within Him until the Flesh became Spirit, you know, so that the grave couldn't hold him! He overcame gravitation. And that is the privilege of everyone, for He was the first-born among many brethren.

"FATHER DIVINE is the Lamb that was slain before the foundation of the world, and HE is the Sacrifice that has destroyed that concept of death. And HE consumed in HIS Body our iniquities; and if we can believe it, we should not have an ache and we should not have a pain if we harmonize with HIM and believe.

"Now FATHER DIVINE said that when they see the GOD of all Creation, they see that Appearance. Now FATHER DIVINE would not be GOD if HE didn't have the Victory over death—if HE couldn't raise that Body—because if GOD is GOD, nothing is greater than GOD, and GOD cannot be limited! But whether HE will do it or not—that's HIS Business. And to those of us who know FATHER DIVINE is GOD, that doesn't say HE'S not GOD. It doesn't add to it, and it doesn't take from it! To us, HE'S Changeless Perfection!

"But I will say this, HE came in a Body, and we can see HIM now if we attune ourselves to HIM. HE has a Body, you know, like I say—if you would raise your consciousness, you can see, and many do see FATHER.

"I believe that the world is going to see FATHER DIVINE again but the main thing for ME and for everyone is to get the reality of HIS Ever Presence, because that's what HE came to bring us—the Consciousness of HIS Ever Presence, as we heard in that Message today—what the Consciousness of GOD'S Ever Presence will do for us. It is the Key that will unlock the Heaven's Door—just the recognition of GOD—because it sets in motion the creative forces of nature. So, without our seeing FATHER Personally, we must see HIM by living at all times in HIS Actual Presence. You understand?"

Professor: (laughing with MOTHER) "I'm trying to."

MOTHER DIVINE: "So it's not a case of waiting like Christianity is waiting. You know, CHRIST would have appeared much sooner if they would have done what Jesus told them to do, you know? CHRIST did come—the Messiah did come to the Jews—but because they didn't really prepare themselves, they didn't know HIM when HE came! And just like FATHER DIVINE is the Second Coming of CHRIST; but Christianity is still waiting for Him. It's a state of consciousness. FATHER DIVINE could come again and people wouldn't know that HE came again, maybe, if they are not in a place to receive HIM! So it's up to the individual. CHRIST is here and now! FATHER DIVINE IS GOD!"

THE NEW DAY, September 18, 1971, pp. 6-7

CHAPTER 9

The Name — "REVEREND M. J. DIVINE"

BECAUSE OF THE PRACTICE of some news media repeating misinformation stored in their news files and continuously carried as authentic background material for current articles, this letter by FATHER DIVINE to "The Answer Man" and the material following in Chapter 10, regarding the use of the false name, George Baker, as applied to FATHER DIVINE, are presented here as the truth of the matter, and as a rebuttal to the lies that have been published. The letter from the Library of Congress puts an end to the wanton use of the false name by libraries in their catalogs and by journalists in their writing.

FATHER DIVINE Declares to Bruce Chapman,
of Radio Program "THE ANSWER MAN,"
"MY NAME IS MAJOR J. DIVINE"

PEACE

764-772 Broad Street
Philadelphia 46, Pennsylvania
November 18, 1946 A.D.F.D.

Mr. Bruce Chapman
145 West 41st Street
New York 18, New York

Dear Mr. Chapman:

Your letter of the 15th ultimo to Mr. Job Paul, Trustee of the Unity Mission Church, Home and Training School, Incorporated, has been received and turned over to ME for reply, and I write in response to same.

Firstly, it was MY understanding that the policy of "The Answer Man" is to state facts, and therefore, I would like to ascertain definitely from whence cometh the source of your answers concerning ME? Certainly you did not question ME to get first-hand information—the truth! But since you have been properly informed by Mr. Job Paul, one of the millions of MY followers, that your statement regarding MY Name is false and untrue, and since, as you say, you believe firmly in the Golden Rule, I request you to not only correct your files but to retract your statement over the air, that your misinformed public might also get the truth.

MY Name is MR. MAJOR J. DIVINE as a civilian and citizen of the United States; but as a Minister of the Gospel, REVEREND MAJOR J. or M. J. DIVINE, better known as FATHER DIVINE, as the Creator, Establisher and Demonstrator of the FATHER DIVINE Peace Mission Movement, and as the Founder and Establisher of many incorporated churches under the Peace Mission Movement, the Cooperative System, and the Righteous Government Department and its Platform under the Peace Mission Movement, and known throughout the world as FATHER DIVINE; but not at any time in the history of MY Personal existence have I ever been called George Baker with MY knowledge of it until recent years in the Mineola case, when with perjured testimonies and affidavits, someone brought that name, unknown to ME before then, into the court.

Notwithstanding those findings, the decision and sentence were reversed by the Appellate Division of the Supreme Court of the State of New York on thirty-two counts of prejudice!

Yet there are those who are malicious, with prejudice and jealousy, who desire to endorse the false, perjured testimonies and affidavits that have long since been ruled out. They desire to do it for the purpose of lowration, distortion and in the act of perverting the minds of the public concerning ME; but I know any democratic and unbiased person will call any other person by the name or names by which they are called, especially by the name by which they call themselves. I call you and all other persons by the name by which you are called; at least, by the name you are known by; but if I were malicious, prejudiced, bigoted, bias-minded towards a person, I might try to call that person by the name that would tend to lowrate or discredit the person of whom I was speaking.

MY Name has never at any time been George Baker, as stated by you and many others who have filled the press and the air with radio broadcasts with false, erroneous and perjured testimonies endorsed as though they were true.

I hope this will give you definite first-hand information so that you might have a chance to be even as this leaves ME, for this leaves ME Well, Healthy, Joyful, Peaceful, Lively, Loving, Success-ful, Prosperous and Happy in Spirit, Body and Mind and in every organ, muscle, sinew, joint, limb, vein and bone and even in every ATOM, fibre and cell of MY Bodily Form.

Respectfully and Sincere, I AM

s/ REV. M. J. DIVINE
(Better known as FATHER DIVINE)

REV.MJD:d

P.S. It is true the decision was legally reversed, as above stated, on thirty-two counts of prejudice, but MY Spirit had already reversed Judge Smith's prejudicial and unjust decision, when he dropped dead with a heart attack in less than five days after sentencing ME. He thought he could stop ME, but MY Spirit removed him.

REV. M.J.D., Ms. D., D.D.

United States Government, Through the Library of Congress
Outlaws the False Name, George Baker, as a Heading for
FATHER DIVINE in the Library of Congress Catalog

UNITED STATES GOVERNMENT   LIBRARY OF CONGRESS

Memorandum   DATE: March 26, 1982

TO: Mother Divine

FROM: Ben R. Tucker, Chief, Officer for
             Descriptive Cataloging Policy

SUBJECT: The Library of Congress heading
             for Father Divine

The Library of Congress heading created in 1936 for Father Divine
under the spurious name "George Baker" has been corrected. Our
heading now reads

Father Divine

The change was initiated in 1979 and is being reflected on all
records going into our new catalog that we began in January, 1981.
This means that as of this date, March 26, 1982, there will be no
further uses of the spurious name as a heading for Father Divine.

s/ Ben R. Tucker

CHAPTER 10

Deliberate Misrepresentation By the Press

Secretary to FATHER DIVINE Assails New York Paper for
Deliberate Misrepresentation of the Truth Concerning
the Peace Mission Movement in a Series of Articles

PEACE

1887 Madison Avenue
New York City
August 4, 1936 A.D.F.D.

Mr. Harvey Deuell
Managing Editor
The Daily News
New York City

My dear Mr. Deuell:

This is a demand for Righteousness, Truth and Justice in the treatment accorded FATHER DIVINE and HIS Movement in the series of articles which is now appearing in your publication. *The Daily News* has had the reputation of being in sympathy with the masses and upholding anything which benefits the under-privileged. Here is a definite instance, I am sure, where in the opinion of thousands who have learned of it, and in the estimation of millions who will know of it, that policy will be considered to have been deliberately reversed.

Lest my judgment should have been considered biased in the matter, I submitted without comment, the first two articles in this series to two unbiased professional persons of intelligence, for their opinions. The response of each was that he considered practically every word of the article hostile. I have requested Mr. Carl Warren, the writer of the articles, to publish a retraction or qualification of his statements and he has failed to do so. Now I am calling upon you, as his superior, to publish this letter with your very next article. If this is not done, we can only conclude that *The Daily News* wishes to be unfair.

The whole trend of your articles published so far in this series — and this applies to only the first two — would be to cast a shadow of ignorance, mystery, heathen superstition, and sinister financial motives, over a Movement which is uplifting wide masses of the people, and unquestionably producing the truest form of Christianity as well as the purest form of Americanism existent in the world today.

FATHER DIVINE TEACHES PUREST CHRISTIANITY

I defy anyone to find anything in FATHER DIVINE'S Teachings or HIS Work that is not exactly in accord with the Life and Teachings of JESUS THE CHRIST as recorded in the four Gospels, or taught and practiced according to the Holy Bible from the time of Moses down to the present time. It is the purest Christianity and the highest form of spirituality known to the world today, and it has been so admitted by many who are leaders in these fields. If it is considered by some to be superstition, remember that in Moses' time people looked to a brazen serpent for deliverance.

So far as the financial aspect of FATHER DIVINE'S Movement is concerned, it is a matter of record that the Disciples of CHRIST had all things in common. There is nothing strange or illegitimate about that. Today, FATHER DIVINE'S followers own their properties cooperatively and operate them as they please. Though in the days of the early Christian Church the people were required to bring their wealth and lay it at the feet of the Apostles, and when Ananias and Sapphira brought only a part of theirs they were struck dead, FATHER DIVINE does not permit such. HIS followers own their own properties and do with them as they please, and if anyone pays any money, it is for actual material value received, and plenty of it.

FATHER DIVINE PRODUCES TRUE AMERICAN CITIZENS

Furthermore, it has been declared by men of unimpeachable reputation who are in a position to know the facts, that no religious or educational institution in the Country is turning out better citizens from the point of view of true Americanism, than FATHER DIVINE is producing.

Ignoring all of this, you have published, under a caption stating that *The Daily News* has dug out the facts, a compilation of allegations, rumors, hearsay, insinuations and information from court records long since repudiated, and admitted by the judge at the time to be unverified; and you have put them forth as positive statements backed by *The Daily News*. The decision of Judge Smith in the case of FATHER DIVINE at Mineola, New York, including the name attributed to FATHER DIVINE and all the charges that went with it, was reversed by the Appellate Division of the Supreme Court of the State of New York, in thirty-two counts of prejudice. The same is true of all charges brought against the followers of FATHER DIVINE at Sayville. The decision was reversed by Appellate Court in the cases of all who did not plead guilty. This places *The Daily News* in the position of digging up information obtained by Judge Smith from malicious and disgruntled persons, which has since been branded by five judges of the Appellate Division as prejudicial, unfounded and untrue, and presenting it again as the truth.

Much of the other information you published is taken almost word for word from books and papers not sufficiently credible to be now in print. Much of it comes also from court records of suits brought against FATHER DIVINE which would not hold water and have never come to trial, or have been dropped long ago. It is a well known fact that many groundless suits are brought against persons of wealth or fame, and that any kind of allegations, no matter how untrue, may be made in such suits.

SAME WORK DONE FOR OVER FORTY YEARS

Mr. Carl Warren, your writer, was warned of this. He was told that witnesses could be produced who had been present with FATHER DIVINE personally for the past forty or fifty years, who could refute practically all of these statements and allegations. He did not see fit to check up on this source of accurate information, but published the untrue statements apparently because it satisfied his mind and served his purpose better. The only slight exception to this was where he said that FATHER DIVINE had denied under oath, the name attributed to HIM, and that there were those who had been with FATHER DIVINE for the past forty to fifty years who declared that HE had been doing the same work during that time.

As evidence of the inaccuracy of all these reports, let me point out to you just one slight instance. This is an easy one for you to check up, as it is of recent date and there is legal record of it. In his second article Mr. Warren stated that the Federal Government had conducted an investigation of FATHER DIVINE'S Activities some time ago and filed some thirty liens against HIS followers for collection of income taxes, but had been able to collect only three thousand dollars—barely enough to cover the cost of collection. As a matter of fact there were seventy-eight liens filed, and the Government collected not one single penny on any of them. After a thorough investigation and many hearings, the cases were completely dropped and documents bearing the seal of the United States Government can be produced to prove this. What do you suppose was the purpose of this misrepresentation? This is typical. It is only an example of a partial untruth, however. Many of the statements are wholly untrue, and this is just as susceptible of proof.

I telephoned Mr. Warren yesterday and asked him to present with the next installment of this series, a statement as to the unreliable sources from which he had gathered his information, and a further statement that his statements were denied by followers of FATHER DIVINE who have had personal knowledge of such matters over a long period of years. He said he would take this under consideration and might possibly publish it with the second article, but this has not been done.

PUBLISH THE TRUTH FOR THE PEOPLE

It is immaterial to FATHER DIVINE or to any of HIS true and faithful followers, what is said one way or the other. As the Movement advances, as it certainly will advance, and as the truth of FATHER DIVINE comes forth more and more, as it certainly will come forth, public opinion will override this false evaluation by *The Daily News* of FATHER DIVINE and HIS Work, and the paper will lose prestige and circulation, just as other papers have done when the public lost confidence in them.

However, in the interest of Righteousness, Truth and Justice, and for the benefit of humanity generally through a better understanding of FATHER DIVINE'S Work, I am asking that you publish this letter with your next article, and just as prominently as you placed the false information, since you apparently do not wish to make a retraction yourselves. Otherwise we shall conclude that you just wish to be unfair, and automatically *The Daily News* will fall into the classification of a certain chain of newspapers FATHER DIVINE'S followers, as well as many other right-thinking people, have resolved never again to buy, read, or have anything to do with, until their policy is changed.

Sincerely,

s/ John Lamb

Validity of Existing Writings on FATHER DIVINE

NON-FOLLOWERS NOT QUALIFIED
TO WRITE ON FATHER DIVINE

In the interest of those contemplating writing on FATHER DIVINE and the Peace Mission Movement, as well as those reading material already published but not authorized or not endorsed by FATHER and MOTHER DIVINE, the following thoughts of FATHER DIVINE are herewith set forth:

"Men come from far and near trying to get the biography or write the history of GOD. The finite wisdom and understanding of man cannot define GOD and cannot write a true history of HIM, for from whence came that wisdom of theirs? Therefore, the limited mortal version of man cannot bind the Omniscience of GOD, and cannot measure GOD with the measure of finite man.

"GOD is infinite by nature, and who can rightfully and accurately write GOD'S History? Who has a mind sufficent to cover the infiniteness of the Infinite One? Who has wisdom to fathom and explain and understand the Omniscience of the Omniscient One?"

From a Message by FATHER DIVINE on May 19, 1943, spoken directly after giving an interview to a young man who wanted to write HIS biography, published in *The New Day* of May 27, 1943, page 17.

WRITERS CANNOT SEE TRUTH UNLESS BORN OF IT

Excerpt from an interview on June 22, 1948, granted by FATHER DIVINE to one who wanted to write on the Peace Mission Movement, published in *The New Day* of July 3, 1948, page 12.

Writer: "I would like to interpret it [The Peace Mission] YOU see, from an outsider looking in."

FATHER: "Well, that is the thought of it. That is where they get all mixed up and misinterpret; because GOD is HIS Own Interpreter and GOD alone can make it plain; not from a Personal point of view necessarily, but from an impersonal point of view, from a psychological point of view; from a mental and spiritual point of view. That is the real way to get the true Message. But when individuals desire—in the which the most of the newspaper men do—desire to get something from their personal point of view, and as you say, from your viewpoint or from their viewpoint, you cannot see the significance of the Truth when you are not a part of it.

". . . it cometh not by sight nor with sight nor with hearing but with a righteous judgment. It is better revealed than told. You can get more first-hand information by being a partaker of the Spirit and Nature of it. You can even, from a physiological or from a traditional or, I might say, from an organizational point of view, one can get messages or get the more definite information by their own experience, through being awakened into that light of whatsoever they are representing."

Writer: "Well now, don't YOU think I might be able to achieve that by visiting the Missions, by partaking in the activities and observing?"

FATHER: "Well, by partaking more of the—yes the activities—that is true in one sense of word—but mainly I stress to be a partaker of the internality of it and not just the physical structure of the demonstrated organization."

Writer: "Well then, isn't it—it is not possible then, to interpret the spirit of the Movement from the outside?"

FATHER: "Well, the Spirit is better interpreted by the Spirit. . . . you would need to be converted, the same as all others would need to be, to get the real significance of the Truth, because the Spirit of the Truth will teach you or will reveal to you the Truth more effectively than what I would tell you Personally—what I would tell you MYSELF Personally. . . .

"I find lots of people for many years, for more than—well, I need not say how many years—but for many, many years the different writers have striven to write ME up with their viewpoint, as to what they see; and what they see cannot be the Truth unless they are born of the Truth. . . .

"It has been the experience of so many who sought it — they did not get it because they did not seek it conscientiously and sincerely and sympathetically. They did not seek it from a spiritual point of view, but they merely sought it from a literary point of view."

NO MAN COULD BE FAIR

> Dr. Charles Braden, author of *These Also Believe* (MacMillan, 1948), which contains a chapter on FATHER DIVINE, was granted an interview with FATHER DIVINE on August 4, 1945. An excerpt from this interview, appearing in *The New Day* of August 11, 1945, page 20, follows.

FATHER: "The thought of it is, it is unfortunate but I doubt whether I would be in a position to cooperate with anyone in writing a book in reference to ME. . .

"A person should not write unless they are unbiased, absolutely unbiased and at a place in consciousness where they could and would receive the Spirit of your Humble Servant. You can learn; as I often say to many other writers, they cannot write of ME rightfully saving by MY Spirit. They can write prejudicially, they can write critically and they can write antagonistically and slanderously and in different ways, but not democratically, because the Spirit of HIM of Whom you may write must present the picture more explicitly than what HE HIMSELF could tell it. . ."

Professor Braden: ". . . there have been some books written about YOU and I read everything I could find. Still I wanted to see YOU and ask, do YOU feel YOU were misrepresented in a number of those books?"

FATHER: "Why, no man could be fair . . . . the only way to write of a person is to partake of that person's spirit . . . the same as a real F.B.I. or any other secret service agent — let that person be a partaker of the nature and characteristics and the habits and customs, rules and regulations of such persons they are anticipating reproducing, and that person will be in a better position to reproduce them characteristically and dispositionally than anyone else who has not made the rightful mental and spiritual contact. . .

"I found as I continued to unfold to the public that I could not give them perfection through the literary world of expression."

CO-AUTHORS AND READERS OF
A CERTAIN BOOK ARE CURSED

Referring to the many newspapers which carried book reviews of FATHER DIVINE — Holy Husband (Doubleday, 1953), by Sarah Harris and Harriet Crittenden, FATHER DIVINE said in a Message which HE gave on November 13, 1953, and which was published in The New Day of November 21, 1953, page 5:

"All of those who carry the article of that book, they shall be cut off. This is Judgment Day! And all who read it shall be cut off, together with it and with them. Aren't you glad! I mean, Mrs. Harris' book! The one that came and got some information from the Church and from MY representatives and then went out to take every lying testimony, every libelous and slanderous statement that has ever been made, concerning ME; tried to find it and publicize it! Now she is cursed! Naturally she is cursed! I mean, I curse her. I, in the Name of Almighty GOD! . . . and you have declared I AM GOD. . . . I curse her and world without end—until the world shall never end. And all who sympathize with her and the publisher, and all of the publishers—I say, I GOD, curse you down! Yes, I curse you!—all who sympathize and harmonize with you; and all who desire to live will discontinue their publications — discontinue reading their publications! If they desire to live, they will do it!

"For I have set before you, this day, a blessing and a cursing—life and death! And those who desire life, they will follow in the wake of the Spirit of Life; and those who think they can ignore this prophecy and prediction, declaration and reiteration of the Scriptures, they may go on and think they can—but they shall be cut off on every hand, in the fulfillment of the Scripture! I have declared it!

"To those who believe sincerely and are living in the Spirit of Meekness and Obedience, in all sincerity as I have been telling you, I say, 'International Peace—in the Air, on Land, on the Sea.' I AM giving you this International Peace! If you would be in the wake of all of the aggressor nations' machine guns and bombs and everything that they may claim to have to destroy the lives of the children of men, I have said, 'International Peace—in the Air, on Land, on the Sea,' for all of those who believe in ME and live according to MY Teaching."

TODAY THE EARTH IS FULFILLING SCRIPTURE

The following Scripture verses enumerate the Blessings that fall on those who keep GOD'S Commandments, as well as the cursings that befall those who do not obey HIS Commandments, as found in Deuteronomy 28:1-46.

> "And it shall come to pass, if thou shalt hearken diligently unto the voice of the LORD thy God, to observe and to do all his commandments which I command thee this day, that the LORD thy God will set thee on high above all nations of the earth:
> "And all these blessings shall come on thee, and overtake thee, if thou shalt hearken unto the voice of the LORD thy God.
> "Blessed shalt thou be in the city, and blessed shalt thou be in the field."

Thereafter are listed the blessings of abundance, health, protection, success and prosperity in detail in verses 4 through 13.

"But it shall come to pass, if thou wilt not hearken unto the voice of the LORD thy God, to observe to do all his commandments and his statutes which I command thee this day; that all these curses shall come upon thee and overtake thee.

"Cursed shalt thou be in the city, and cursed shalt thou be in the field."

In verses 17 through 46 are listed the curses of lacks, wants and limitations, oppression, sickness and finally death which are predestined to come upon the unbelievers who disobey GOD.

CHAPTER 11

Cause of Disasters

Prejudice and Inequality Cited by FATHER DIVINE
in the Following Two Letters Are the
Cause of Airline and Other Disasters

PEACE

764-772 Broad Street
Philadelphia 46, Pennsylvania
June 12, 1947 A.D.F.D.

Dr. Edward Warner
President, International Civil Airlines Organization (I.C.A.O)
1529 McGregor Street
Montreal, Quebec, Canada

Dear Dr. Warner:

It has been brought to my attention that you are the President of the I.C.A.O., an International Airlines Organization, and that there are and have been many different disasters in connection with the airline transportation, through which many lives have been blotted out, even to the most recent crashes here in the States.

At the La Guardia Field, Thursday night, May 29th, 1947, some forty-two persons were killed and on May the 30th, Decoration Day at Port Deposit, Maryland, a plane crashed, destroying and mutilating beyond identification, some fifty-three persons; and many other such disasters have occurred in the aviation field of science. Investigations have been made and no doubt, the whole field of aviation technic is under investigation. Apparently, they cannot find the cause for these crashes and disasters in the field of science.

PREJUDICE, DIVISION AND STRIFE

It is a definite fact that your concern, of which you are in control, is motivated by prejudice, division and strife. That, as I have long since declared, will cause the airplanes not to stay in the air. It is written:

"Where there is division, there is strife";

and it is also written:

"Divided we fall."

Therefore Dr. Warner, I appeal to you, as the representative of a great international enterprise, to take steps immediately to bring an end to all segregation and discrimination and prejudice and selfishness in your field of study, of science and invention; and immediately demand the enactment of the Bill of Rights of the Constitution of the United States of America, with equity and justice to be executed accurately in every activity in business, profession, labor and trade and in every field of activity, even domestically, socially; and even in your immediate lineage, institute equity and justice and impregnate the minds of all of the subjects of those with whom you are concerned, with equity and equality for everybody, so that by these means, in keeping with our great national statesman, Abraham Lincoln, the subjects of all of these enterprises and institutions might have a New Birth of Freedom, even the whole nation and our civilization, that such governing forces and the authorities of the authorities and the governments and controlling authorities of these enterprises and institutions with which we are concerned, might not perish from the earth.

REASON FOR DISASTERS

For without a new birth of Freedom from all racism, sectarianism, Fascism, barbarism, Nazism, Hitlerism and all other divisions of segregation, Jim-Crowism, as it is called, as well as all of the selfish, discriminatory practices of men, being brought to an abolition, this government and those fundamentals upon which you lean, will perish from the earth, for such cannot continue to have access in the land, for the LORD reigneth and truly,

"Righteousness and judgment are the habitation of his throne."

Psalms 97:2

The many tornadoes, floods, hurricanes, earthquakes, volcanoes and other storms, as the cosmic forces of nature, do work havocly and go forth rampant in the land where wickedness, vice and crime abound.

Therefore, as I have aforesaid, the airplanes will not stay in the air and a good many of them will continue to refuse to leave the ground, motivated by prejudice, division, selfishness and strife, for the Mouth of the LORD has declared it! Trains will not stay on the track and ships will not stay on the ocean filled and controlled with and by prejudice, division, racism, Nazism, Fascism and strife, with all of those detestable tendencies of men that try to destroy and put some up and some down, all because of the color of their skins and because of their racial or national origin.

Yet, there are many good-thinking and just persons who are made subject to vanity unwittingly, and at times, forced into tolerating, condoning and endorsing segregation, discrimination and oppression, such as has caused the lives of millions to be destroyed.

AN APPEAL FOR JUSTICE

Therefore, unto you and unto all officials and executives of these great enterprises and even to the national and international traffic commission and all representatives and to each of our great national governments and their representatives, I do appeal and request the honor of your office, your official and executive duty and authority, to put into action every ounce of your energy, your authority, minds and attention in eradicating these terrible vices and crimes against humanity that have caused the loss of the lives of millions.

When the nations of the earth were ignoring Mussolini's acts of aggression, I contacted him by communication, protesting his invasion of Ethiopia. He ignored MY request. Later, Virginio Gayda, his mouthpiece, publicly announced according to radio and press reports, that the United States could never be the leader for the other nations of the earth because of "FATHER DIVINE and HIS fifty million followers." Mussolini might have been alive today had he taken cognizance of MY Message to him, but no doubt he may have thought I was foolish. Yet it is written:

"The foolishness of God is wiser than men; and the weakness of God is stronger than men." I Corinthians 1:25

Even back in 1932 and '33 I petitioned representatives of government to bring an end to the oppresson, suppression and persecution of the Jews in Germany and in all other countries, but they did not take cognizance of it. To ward off the invasion of Czechoslovakia and the onslaught of inhuman warfare, I petitioned the various heads of government by cablegram:

"Why not propose purchase of coveted Czechoslovakian territory, with Sudetens helping to pay for annexation, substituting cooperation and Peace for terrible inhuman warfare consequences?"

There were many different proposals I made so that our civilization and these democracies in which we live might be saved the cost in lives, in money and in resources, of another inhuman war, but they did not take cognizance of them.

COST OF WORLD WAR II

Toward the conclusion of MY proposals that were made for National and International Defense, I also proposed the unification of the Three Americas, which would have been much easier than the cost to humanity of the twenty-two million, sixty thousand estimated killed plus the injured and the one trillion, one hundred fifty-four billion dollars in armament military materials, plus the property damage estimated at more than two hundred thirty billion, nine hundred million dollars.

When I proposed the unification of the Three Americas, many asked where we would get the money from to make all of the Americas One Democracy; but where did the United States get the three hundred seventeen billion, six hundred million dollars expended for war materials alone, by the United States? Such a unification might not only have saved this Nation and the Allied Nations such great expense, but it might have arrested the Axis Nations from continuing in the way of aggression and thus saved them from destroying millions of their own subjects and spending an estimated four hundred sixty-eight billion, nine hundred thirty-nine million dollars in war materials and the total destruction of property in some areas, many times greater even than the destruction in England, according to the authorities.

Yet, all of this could have been avoided had they taken cognizance of MY Message; but because of prejudice, bigotry, racism, Hitlerism, Fascism and all of the isms combined, such as I have aforementioned, that create division and strife and cause the loss of millions of lives, they failed to hearken unto MY Voice.

RETRIBUTION IS SURE!

The cosmic forces of nature, the creative forces and even Nature itself, work destructively because of prejudice and bigotry. There is no escape for prejudice and division, for retribution is sure and retribution is assured for crime does not pay!

Just think of all of the Axis Governments, how the empires they had built went down in defeat by continuing their prejudice, division and strife, propagating and advocating racism, in short, races, creeds and colors. And not only the governments were defeated but even the representatives of those respective governments which have fallen, for the crimes they committed, many have been executed. They are held responsible for the atrocious crimes committed by their governments when they were in authority.

I hope the whole world will take cognizance of these thoughts I have conveyed, as well as all who are concerned, for unless they all, who are filled with prejudice, division and strife of any kind, repent and turn from their sins, they shall also in the like manner perish.

As with a state or community, so with a nation; and as with a nation or country, as mentioned, so with a state or community or an organization and all of its representatives.

CITIZENS DENIED FREE ACCESS TO PROPERTY

Men seek to segregate themselves and place restrictions on deeds and papers and other supposedly legitimate contracts and agreements, for the purpose of prohibiting the free access of all citizens to buy property and to live wheresoever they choose, and by such prejudice, division and strife, by making such restrictions in such agreements and contracts and deeds and titles, the very ground itself is cursed, for it is written:

"It shall come to pass, if thou wilt not hearken unto the voice of the LORD thy God, to observe to do all his commandments and his statutes which I command you this day; that all these curses shall come upon thee, and overtake thee:

"Cursed shalt thou be in the city, and cursed shalt thou be in the field.

"Cursed shall be thy basket and thy store.

"Cursed shall be the fruit of thy body, and the fruit of thy land, the increase of thy kine, and the flocks of thy sheep.

"Cursed shalt thou be when thou comest in, and cursed shalt thou be when thou goest out." Deuteronomy 28:15-19

INCREASING DESTRUCTION OF LIFE

Then I say, you can see why floods and storms and hurricanes and tornadoes and fire, pestilence and disasters are destroying the lives of increasing numbers, for of those who refuse to hearken unto the Voice of GOD, it is written:

"His children are far from safety, and they are crushed in the gate, neither is there any to deliver them." Job 5:4

Where prejudice, division, bigotry and strife exist, disaster also exists or follows and the Texas City fire, the floods in the Middle West and the many airplane crashes, train wrecks and automobile wrecks attest this fact; for as with a nation, so with an individual, and as with a place locally, in any locality, so with a nation universally.

Then I say, I hope that all who are concerned, as well as all mankind, will take cognizance of this Message, for I have made this appeal not for any benefit that I may derive as a Person, but that millions of lives may yet be saved, even as I desired to save the twenty-two million, sixty thousand lives reported dead by this last great inhuman World War; for without a change of heart and mind and characteristics through a New Birth of Freedom under GOD, for which Abraham Lincoln prayed and which I have come to bring, mankind cannot hope to become to be even as this leaves ME, as I AM Well, Healthy, Joyful, Peaceful, Lively, Loving, Successful, Prosperous and Happy in Spirit, Body and Mind and in every organ, muscle, sinew, joint, limb, vein and bone and even in every ATOM, fibre and cell of MY Bodily Form.

Respectfully and Sincere, I AM

s/ REV. M. J. DIVINE
(Better known as FATHER DIVINE)

REV. MJD/r

P.S. This is an open letter, and a copy to be sent to the International Traffic Commission and other representatives in federal and state government, so that they may be able to ascertain the cause of these great disasters, such as the different airplane crashes as mentioned in the body of this letter.

REV. M.J.D.

STUYVESANT REFUSES N - - - - HOST'S RENT
(News clipping followed by pertinent letter)

The Metropolitan Life Insurance Company has returned the September rent check of union organizer Jesse Kessler, who permitted a N - - - - family to use his Stuyvesant Town apartment.

The company, which won a suit seeking to force it to rent to N - - - - s, charged Mr. Kessler had violated his lease by "permitting others to occupy your apartment."

The N - - - - family, Mr. and Mrs. Hardine Hendrix and their son, 5, meanwhile have moved into another apartment in Stuyvesant Town because the Kessler family returned from vacation. They were provided with an apartment by Dr. Lee Lorch, former City College Instructor.

128

PEACE

764-772 Broad Street
Philadelphia 46, Pennsylvania
September 19, 1949 A.D.F.D.

Mr. Leroy A. Lincoln, President
Metropolitan Life Insurance Company
1 Madison Avenue
New York, New York

Mr dear Mr. Lincoln:

MY attention has been called to an act of discrimination by the organization of which you are the President, the Metropolitan Life Insurance Company, which has refused to rent apartments to Afro-American citizens in your Stuyvesant Town apartments in New York City.

I AM writing to you, as an organizational father, that those under you and affiliated with you might escape the disasters that follow in the wake of prejudice, discrimination, bigotry and segregation. When you segregate in the Northern Middle Atlantic States and in a State that has passed the FEPC Bill and the Civil Rights Bill, all evidences reflect as if though you desire to endorse segregation and discrimination, which bring on such disasters as have claimed the lives of millions in recent years.

The Law of GOD is Universal and when men segregate and try to prohibit some of their fellowmen from enjoying the same rights and privileges because of prejudice, bigotry, division and strife, they automatically bring upon themselves the wrath of GOD. Hence, I appeal to you, even as I appealed to Dr. Edward Warner, the President of the International Civil Airlines Organization (I.C.A.O.) to use every ounce of your energy, your authority and influence to eradicate all prejudice, division and segregation from

129

every branch of your company; for I do not desire to see happen again, such disasters as the Winecoff Hotel fire in Atlanta, Georgia, on December 7th, 1946, when one hundred twenty-one were killed.

PREJUDICE CAUSES UNTOLD LOSSES

It may sound like foolishness, but had Adolf Hitler taken cognizance of MY Message to him before the start of the most inhuman World War II, it would have saved the forty-five million, two hundred thirty-three thousand, four hundred thirty-six lives that have been recorded killed and missing from the latest available records, as well as the expenditure of hundreds of billions of dollars in war materials, not to mention the total property destroyed.

It is not a supposition. It looks terrible in the European countries where thousands and thousands are starving there. The transgressions and iniquities of their political fathers, by being converted into Hitlerism, Fascism and their doctrines of prejudice, segregation, hatred and division, have been visited upon them. Yet, the same identical doctrine which Hitler propagated, is being propagated by the company of which you are the organizational father. However, the same GOD is alive today who visited the iniquities of Hitler, Mussolini, Tojo and their associates on them and on their political offsprings, organizational offsprings, and even their physical natural children, as it is written:

> "I the LORD thy God am a jealous God, visiting the iniquity of the fathers upon the children unto the third and fourth generation of them that hate me,
> "And shewing mercy unto thousands of them that love me and keep my commandments." Deuteronomy 5:9,10

You can see, read and hear every day, numerous accounts of the iniquities of the parents which are visited upon them and their children; for acts of prejudice, bigotry, segregation and intolerance

130

have preceded such tragedies as the terrible fire in the Cocoanut Grove night club in Boston on November 28, 1942, in which four hundred ninety-one were killed and over two hundred injured.

That is just one of many of which you, no doubt, are aware. There was the fire in the Gulf Hotel in Houston, Texas, September 7th, 1943 in which scores were injured and forty-nine killed. Prior to many such tragedies, I had Personally warned those in charge to discontinue their acts of prejudice, segregation and discrimination.

BEACHES CURSED BY DISCRIMINATION

It has been something like it was in 1917 when Mother Divine and I went down to Rockaway Beach and ordered bath houses. They said, "You can't get a bath house here," or words to that effect. That was at a public beach, but they thought the water was too good for ME to go into; however, I said, "If WE cannot go in, nobody else will go in!" Shortly after that, tar came up in the water at Rockaway Beach as never before and spoiled the whole season.

A similar incident occurred in Miami in 1947, when some of MY followers who happened to be of a dark complexion, wanted to go in bathing in Miami, but the authorities would not allow them to go on the beach or into the water and threatened to have them put into jail, even though they did allow dogs to go in the water. They wrote ME about the incident and within a few days, tons of dead fish came up in the water and were washed ashore on the Florida beaches for miles and miles, and there was such a stench the people could not stand it and the beaches were deserted. Bathing was impossible. Millions of dollars were reported lost by resort owners, and the cost of digging ditches to bury the dead fish was tremendous. They called it the "Red Tide" but whatsoever the scientific cause, the real mental and spiritual cause was prejudice, segregation and division.

The very same prejudice was displayed in New York State of a recent date, when Mother and I and some of MY Staff went as guests of one of the residents of Sayville, down to the beach to look at the Great South Bay. The citizens of Islip township, through their officers, did not want ME and MINE to even look at the Great South Bay. They had signs up, which they said they intended to enforce,

"For the residents of the Township of Islip only."

WE left and within a week, seaweed and stinging jellyfish came up in the Bay, making it impossible for the citizens themselves, to swim in the water. That is not in Florida, but in New York State, that presumably has passed the Civil Rights Bill in its State legislature. But I have warned them, as I AM warning you, to get rid of prejudice and discrimination.

After the Red Tide had deposited tons of dead fish on her beaches, Florida did not cease to discriminate and the hurricane that swept through the State from September 16th to the 19th of 1947, cost the State more than a hundred lives and millions of dollars in property damage, according to statistics.

MANY DISASTERS CITED

The same prejudice brought about the Texas-Oklahoma tornado in April of 1947 in which one hundred sixty-seven were killed and damage reported to property amounting to ten million dollars.

If the former managing editor of *Look* Magazine, Mr. Jack Guenther, who was burned to death in the airplane crash in Bryce Canyon, Utah, in October 1947, in a terrible tragedy which killed fifty-two people—if he could speak he himself could tell you of his own personal prejudice of which I have a definite record.

Your company may have paid out accident insurance to some of the families of the victims of the St. Anthony Hospital fire in which seventy-four persons were killed on April 4th of this year. No doubt, some of the passengers in the plane crash off Puerto Rico, which claimed fifty-three lives in June, or the victims of the crash of the C-46 in Seattle, in which nine were killed and thirty-three others injured, when the plane crashed into an apartment building trapping two persons in the smouldering ruins of the building—no doubt, some of them may have carried Metropolitan Life Insurance policies. At any rate I AM sure you know of the plane crash near Santa Susana Pass in California on July 12th in which thirty-eight were killed and the crash of the Dutch KLM Constellation which crashed near New Delhi, India, killing all forty passengers and crew, including thirteen top American newspaper, magazine and radio correspondents.

The same month on July 30th, sixteen persons were killed when a Navy plane crashed into an Eastern Air Lines passenger plane near Fort Dix, New Jersey and on August 8th, of this year, fifteen passengers were trapped and killed and thirteen others injured in a Greyhound bus crash in Bloomington, Indiana.

These are somewhat minor tragedies compared with the terrible earthquake in Ecuador on August 8th, in which four thousand, six hundred were killed and an estimate of more than twenty millions of dollars' worth of property lost. The typhoon which wiped out American installations on Okinawa and left an estimated twenty million dollars' worth of damage, did not destroy so many lives, but when it reached Shanghai, China, it left two hundred thousand homeless and killed twenty-nine, besides the two who were killed on the island of Okinawa.

Then there was the hurricane last month in Florida which destroyed from twenty to thirty million dollars' worth of citrus fruit alone, not to mention the loss in other property. Also, on August 14th in Australia, the Municipal Council of Kempsey barred all aborigines living in the area from using the town's public swimming pool, and on August 29th in a flash flood, the shopping center of Kempsey was laid waste, bridges destroyed, twenty-two homes were washed away with unestimated damage to public and private property.

Just this month, on September 10th, in Canada, a Canadian Pacific Airlines DC-3 crashed, killing all of its twenty-three passengers and crew. On Friday the 9th, in a raging thunder storm off Nantucket Sound, nine persons, who tried to save themselves by tying themselves together with a rope, when their yacht became swamped by the waves, all drowned and only two of the yacht's passengers were saved.

But the most recent tragedy which is uppermostly in the consideration of the American people is the ill-fated Noronic, which caught fire at a pier in Toronto early Saturday morning, from which, according to the latest report, two hundred five are either dead or missing and of the one hundred eighty-nine injured, sixteen are seriously hurt, all because of prejudice, division, segregation and hatred.

GOD'S LAW ABOVE MAN'S LAW

It may work out the same with the enterprises with which the Metropolitan Life Insurance Company is connected if you and other officials of the Company do not immediately bring an end to your policy of segregation; for even though you may have won a court decision, giving you the legal right to segregate, the Law of GOD is above the laws of men and if men fail to obey GOD, they may think that GOD is indeed public enemy number one!

I have written to you the simple facts of a few disasters. There are many more which I feel assured that you are well aware, and yet of these, every one could have been avoided by the simple enactment of the Laws of GOD, of real Americanism, Brotherhood, Christianity, Democracy and true Judaism, as they are synonymous; for though

"I am visiting the iniquity of the fathers upon the children unto the third and fourth generation of them that hate me;

"Yet I am shewing mercy unto thousands, yea millions, of them that love me, and keep my commandents." Exodus 20:5,6

I know whereof I speak, and therefore, I address this appeal to you and your associates, that through a New Birth of Freedom under GOD, this Nation and its citizens might not perish from the earth because of prejudice, division and strife; for only by a New Birth of Freedom can this people be liberated from racism, segregation and hatred and have the privilege of becoming to be even as this leaves ME, as I AM Well, Healthy, Joyful, Peaceful, Lively, Loving, Successful, Prosperous and Happy in Spirit, Body and Mind and in every organ, muscle, sinew, joint, limb, vein and bone and even in every ATOM, fibre and cell of MY Bodily Form.

Respectfully and Sincere, I AM

s/ REV. M.J. DIVINE, Ms. D., D.D.
(Better known as FATHER DIVINE)

REV. MJD/r

CHAPTER 12

Jim Jones of People's Temple, Guyana

Rev. Jim Jones Cut Down by Retribution;
Takes Hundreds With Him in Death Pact;
Once Sought Control of Peace Mission Movement
(News Clipping)

PHILADELPHIA, NOVEMBER 24, 1978 (DP) The statistics of what promises to be the top news story of the year are all too familiar by now. Rev. Jim Jones, 47, of People's Temple, San Francisco, led hundreds of his members to their deaths in a mass suicide pact at the Jones compound in Guyana, South America, Saturday, November 18, following the killing by his members of Representative Leo J. Ryan and four other Americans. The Congressman was there to investigate repeated reports of beatings, people losing their possessions and mistreatment of children. "Jim Jones used those poor people just like Charlie Manson," Mr. Ryan said.

DESIRED CONTROL OF MOVEMENT

But little known are the facts connected with the overtures of Jones to FATHER DIVINE, MOTHER DIVINE and prominent members of the Peace Mission Movement.

Out of obscurity he and many others like him have come and gone. But none have gone in such a startling and morbid manner. Neither had any the affrontery with which he approached FATHER DIVINE.

During an interview he first had with FATHER at HIS Headquarters here in July, 1958, with MOTHER DIVINE and members of the secretarial staff present, Pastor Jones brazenly made his intent clear, stating he intended to eventually take FATHER'S place.

The contrast was apparent. Jim Jones, self-centered, egotistic and defiant, was at once belittled by the humility and graciousness of FATHER DIVINE.

He visited again the following year and was extended the same hospitality.

PLANNED STRATEGY

In 1965 he offered his services to the Peace Mission Movement in a more subtle way, opening his home and facilities to MOTHER DIVINE and the followers, inviting Her to come should there be war between the nations at a time when there was no threat of war to this country.

By 1971 his method was more true to his aggressive nature. A trip was planned for over 200 of his members, pretending a sincere desire to fellowship with members of the Movement.

On July 23, over 200 adults and children arrived with him from California at the Woodmont estate. For the several days they remained in Philadelphia, the militant attitude of Jones and the leaders of the group became increasingly obvious. His distaste for the government of the United States and the establishment, and the prosperity of the followers in general began to be expressed in casual, then more deliberate remarks he made to MOTHER DIVINE and others.

Finally, Jim Jones and the entire group was asked to leave, the deportment of the adults had become so brazen and obnoxious.

Although the hospitality of FATHER DIVINE had been extended without reserve, the following November, letters were sent to each of the churches, hotels, and homes of the Peace Mission Movement here, inviting followers to come to Rev. Jones, giving the date that buses would be arriving to pick them up.

Other mail began to pour in to everyone as the rally for membership progressed. Writers, anonymous and otherwise, lauded the virtues of Jones, his supposed healings, his "Mount of the House of the Lord" in Ukiah, California, his pronouncements which he now called "Apostolic Socialism."

Little attention was paid to any of it. There was one thing Jim Jones had not reckoned with, the constant Teachings of FATHER DIVINE that with or without a Body HE remains the same and is at all times present. This holds followers steadfast, living continually in the consciousness of HIS Presence, endeavoring to daily live according to the Life of CHRIST.

As the buses arrived, loud speakers blasted out over the streets again offering the invitation to visit the Jones camp free of charge. Leaflets were passed out on the streets by his members. They became a general nuisance and had to be stopped.

A handful were curious enough to take the trip, most of them leaving when they grasped the true intent of this "hospitality" and the method of fear and force used to keep people against their will.

Jones and his wife became known as "Father" and "Mother" Jones.

Periodically, over several years, Rev. Jones personally attempted to draw officials within the Peace Mission Movement who worked closely with FATHER DIVINE, into his fold. Only one of hundreds contacted joined him.

MOTHER DIVINE answered a letter written by this individual to Her in December, 1971. She said in part,

"How can you possibly think that FATHER DIVINE would reincarnate HIMSELF in these last days of mortality in a human likeness, much less in one born in sin and shaped up in iniquity, according to his own testimony and now married, having one child according to the flesh? The Sonship Degree came through a virgin birth and the FATHERSHIP Degree came without the beginning of days or the end of life. . . ."

MOTHER DIVINE'S ULTIMATUM

On July 16, 1972, six years before the Guyana horrors, MOTHER DIVINE'S ultimatum concerning the Jones group was inspired by FATHER DIVINE'S dynamic taped sermon given September 14, 1952, entitled, "If You Are Not Satisfied, Get Something That Satisfies," which had just been played during the Holy Communion Service.

Following the Sermon, after years of patient longsuffering with Jim Jones, MOTHER put a stop to everything—the blatant lies and misrepresentations, the infringement of private rights of citizens, the influx of unwanted correspondence, attempted defamation of character, even his evil attempts to defame the holy and virtuous character of MOTHER Herself, Whom FATHER DIVINE speaks of as HIS Spotless Virgin Bride.

"We have entertained Pastor Jones and the People's Temple," She stated. "We were entertaining angels of the 'other fellow'! (the term followers use to denote the d - v - l) We no longer extend to them any hospitality whatsoever! Not a one of them is welcome in any Church under the jurisdiction of the Peace Mission Movement, here, or in any other Country! They are not welcome in any of our public Hotels; they are not welcome in any of our public dining rooms. They are not welcome!"

HIS DEEDS JUDGED HIM

Now, at 47, Jim Jones is dead—the man who so desperately wanted to be GOD, in whom good was no longer to be found. Had he sincerely desired to bring himself into subjection to the Life of CHRIST as he saw it demonstrated in FATHER DIVINE, he could have led a fruitful career. But because he mocked GOD by self-aggrandizement, his greed for power, the lust of the flesh, the love of money, his anti-American spirit and mind led him to destroy himself and all those who followed him also. Truly is the Scripture fulfilled:

"... for the leaders of the people cause them to err and they that are led of them are destroyed." Isaiah 9:16

So, before the eyes of a shocked world, Jim Jones, the leader who had mocked GOD by trying to use the Power of the Universe selfishly, was obliged to reap the reward of all those who attempt to rob GOD of HIS Glory.

FATHER DIVINE'S Sermon referred to above, MOTHER DIVINE'S Ultimatum, this article, MOTHER DIVINE'S letter in 1971 to a defector, and an article from the *Philadelphia Journal* of November 30, 1978, can be found in *The New Day* of December 9, 1978, pp. 1,12-18.

CHAPTER 13

FATHER DIVINE'S Peace Proposals and Declarations to the United States and Other Governments

THESE PROPOSALS are made into and known as "FATHER DIVINE'S Peace Stamps" (stickers), which are sent out as messages and ambassadors to the world at large, in times of extreme emergency, to bring an end to inhuman warfare, panics and famines, and to bring about Righteousness, Justice, Peace and Unity for all mankind.

PEACE

"PEACE TO THE WORLD AT LARGE"
FATHER DIVINE

Cables to: Chancellor Hitler, Prime Minister Chamberlain, Premier Daladier, Pres. Benes, Pres. Roosevelt, Sept. 20, 1938, A.D.F.D.

"Why not propose purchase of coveted Czechoslovakian territory, with Sudetans helping to pay for annexation, substituting cooperation and Peace for terrible inhuman warfare consequences?"

FATHER DIVINE

——o——

"It is my conviction that all people under the threat of war today pray that Peace may be made before, rather than after war."

PRESIDENT ROOSEVELT

PEACE

ONE NATION

ONE LANGUAGE ' ONE FLAG ONE SPEECH

Telegrams to: Pres. Roosevelt, V. Pres. Garner and U. S. Senate, Hon. Bankhead, House of Representatives, Sec. of State Hull and Sec. of War Woodring, Dec. 9, 1939 A.D.F.D.

"Why not unite the Three Americas as a National and International Defense for Peace? Let there be

THE UNITED COUNTRIES OF AMERICA

even as this is the United States of America; if not I propose that the United States purchase Central and South America, and make all the Americas one Democracy."

FATHER DIVINE

Everybody Buy Bonds!

Jan. 12, 1944 A.D.F.D.

"For victory let all the Allies unite consolidatedly and every American citizen buy Bonds unlimitedly for victory and a just and lasting Peace; and for reconstruction, mass production, rescuing the perishing and to care for the dying.

"The Axis will unconditionally surrender by sending an Ambassage desiring conditions of Peace."

(See St. Luke 14:31,32)

REV. M. J. DIVINE

FOR A JUST AND LASTING PEACE

Why not propose at the International Conference of Nations, the Unification of all the Mutual and Allied Sovereignties of the Universe and let the United Countries of the World be One Big Universal Allied Sovereignty?

By the Unity of Spirit, Mind, Aim and of Purpose, let all of the Allied Sovereignties unite consolidatedly and the Four Freedoms will be made a reality!

July 6, 1944 A.D.F.D.   FATHER DIVINE

PEACE EVERYONE

For Reconversion, Reconstruction and Mass Production, for Universal Unity and Tranquility, for the Peace we must now win, Unite Consolidatedly again, and Buy Bonds Unlimitedly—the Victory of Peace to win. By the Unity of Spirit, of Mind, of Aim and of Purpose we have won the Victory Universally and shall win it from every angle expressible.

To bring an abolition to the possibility of inflation, depressions, panics and famines, let us unite on the Home Front and let there be no division and we will have a perfect Union that is called for by our Constitution, and the Universal Brotherhood of man will be made a living reality.

October 23, 1945 A.D.F.D.   FATHER DIVINE

PEACE EVERYONE

July 1, 1946 A.D.F.D.

Speaker, Hon. Sam Rayburn
Joint Session of Congress
House of Representatives
Washington, D.C.

A greater Memorial by Congress to our late President Franklin Delano Roosevelt, would be the passage of an extension of forceful OPA regulations of Price Control according to the request of our present President Harry S. Truman.

FATHER DIVINE

PEACE EVERYONE

His Excellency, Mr. Trygve Lie
Sec. Gen. of the United Nations
Flushing Manors, Lake Success, N.Y.

Telegram: The UN, Dec. 9, 1946 A.D.F.D.

I repeat my proposal:

I propose that the UN accept of Philadelphia as the capital of the United Countries of the World, as this is the Cradle of Democracy.

Let us establish the Foundation of the Universal Brotherhood of Man and make this the Country Seat of the United Sovereignties of the World!

(Signed) REV. M.J. DIVINE
(Better known as FATHER DIVINE)

June 11, 1947 A.D.F.D.

TO THE PRESIDENT OF THE UNITED STATES OF TODAY:

I appeal to you and every Representative and Senator in accord—for the salvation of yourselves and your subjects here and at large, you had better make laws immediately to bring an end to segregation and discrimination and to bring an end to the rights of states that are unconstitutional to have their Sovereign Rights.

I appeal to the Federal Government and its Representatives to cross the borders of all Sovereign States and break every State Law that is unconstitutional and that will endorse murder, vice and crime such as those of many of the States of the Union. The time is out for that!

REV. M.J. DIVINE, Ms.D.
(Better known as FATHER DIVINE)

PEACE!

"PEACE TO THE WORLD AT LARGE"
FATHER DIVINE

I do hereby this day make this Proclamation, that from now henceforth the twenty-ninth day of April shall be an International, Universal, Interracial Holiday commemorating the Marriage of CHRIST to HIS Creation, yea, GOD to HIS Spotless Church—HIS Spotless Virgin Bride—to Universalize Democracy, Americanism, Christianity and Judaism as Synonymous, and to bring about the Universal Brotherhood of Man and the Propagation of Virtue, Honesty and Truth!

April 29, 1948 A.D.F.D.   REV. M. J. DIVINE, Ms.D., D.D.

INTERNATIONAL PEACE

IN THE AIR . . . ON LAND . . . ON THE SEA

August 6, 1948 A.D.F.D

This is GOD'S Administration, and all Nations, this whole Generation and even our present Civilization shall have a New Birth of Freedom Under GOD, for I declare that Americanism, Brotherhood, Democracy, Christianity and Judaism are Synonymous.

(Signed) REV. M.J. DIVINE
(Better known as FATHER DIVINE)

THE PENDULUM OF EQUILIBRIUM

Hereafter, all nations shall be guided by the Pendulum of Equilibrium which I have started swinging in the Defense of Humanity generally and for the Preservation of Peace Universally.

The Unification of all Nations or Allied Nations is the only Hope of Salvation of any Nation.

April 25, 1949 A.D.F.D.   FATHER DIVINE

March 14, 1950 A.D.F.D.

Office talk comment on the Interracial and International Marriage of the African Prince, Seretse Khama, to English schoolgirl.

By intuition and by scientific geographic inspiration I AM moving in all Nations and I AM bringing all People together. I have broken that line of demarcation, but it is only being shown gradually in the present different demonstrations.

REV. M. J. DIVINE, Ms.D., D.D.
(Better known as FATHER DIVINE)

March 16, 1950 A.D.F.D.

I, by intuition and by inspiration, even though it came through—it came through a deep consideration and consultation of the Chief Executive before it was done, he decided to do it as I inspired him to do—to permit them to make the H-Bomb! Now the Axis or any other aggressor nation that would desire to rise in opposition to this one, with the right concept of common sense, they would know they would be subject to total destruction if they would rise in opposition to this nation.

"For HE is the Minister of GOD to thee for good. But if thou do that which is evil, be afraid: For he beareth not the sword in vain: for he is the Minister of God, a Revenger to execute wrath upon him that doeth evil."

(Romans 13:4)

REV. M. J. DIVINE, Ms.D., D.D.
(Better known as FATHER DIVINE)

UNIFY! UNIFY! UNIFY!

PEACE   May 6, 1950 A.D.F.D.

"I propose that Australia, New Zealand and America unite as one great Nation, having the U. S. Constitution, Declaration of Independence and Bill of Rights, as a means of National and International Defense for Peace and in fulfilment of the Scripture Genesis 11:6:

> *'And the LORD said, Behold the people is one,*
> *and they have all one language; and this they*
> *begin to do: and now nothing will be restrained*
> *from them, which they have imagined to do.' "*

REV. M. J. DIVINE, Ms.D., D.D.
(Better known as FATHER DIVINE)

RETROACTIVE COMPENSATION

PEACE   July 28, 1951 A.D.F.D.

All nations and peoples who have suppressed and oppressed the under-privileged, they will be obliged to pay the African slaves and their descendants for all uncompensated servitude and for all unjust compensation, whereby they have been unjustly deprived of compensation on the account of previous condition of servitude and the present condition of servitude.

This is to be accomplished in the defense of all other under-privileged subjects and must be paid retroactive up-to-date.

REV. M. J. DIVINE, Ms.D., D.D.
(Better known as FATHER DIVINE)

NATIONALIST CHINA

Philadelphia, Penna.

September 14, 1951 A.D.F.D.

Telegrams to — President of the United States
HARRY S. TRUMAN:

"Why not immediately officially accept of Chiang Kai-Shek's Nationalist Government of China and permit Japan to sign a Bilateral Treaty with Chiang Kai-Shek and let them become to be consolidatedly allied with us before he will be forced to join Communist China?"

REV. M. J. DIVINE, Ms.D., D.D.
(Better known as FATHER DIVINE)

September 14, 1951 A.D.F.D.

His Excellency TRYGVE LIE
Secretary General of the United Nations:

"Why not immediately officially accept of Chiang Kai-Shek's Nationalist Government of China permitting them full status with other Allied Nations including Japan and let them become to be consolidatedly allied with us before he will be forced to join Communist China?"

REV. M. J. DIVINE, Ms.D., D.D.
(Better known as FATHER DIVINE)

ACCEPTANCE OF AUSTRALIA AND
NEW ZEALAND
AS STATES OF THE UNITED STATES

May 6, 1950 A.D.F.D.

Joint Session of Congress,
The House of Representatives and
    The United States Senate,
To The Vice-President, President of the Senate,
    Honorable Alben W. Barkley,
and The Speaker of the House,
    Honorable Sam Rayburn

Honorable Sirs:

I have authentic information that Australia desires to unite with the United States and be one of the states of the Union. Therefore, I propose the following:

I PROPOSE THAT THE UNITED STATES ACCEPT AND ADMIT AUSTRALIA AND NEW ZEALAND TO THE UNION, AND ANY OTHER COUNTRY WHICH DESIRES TO UNITE TO THE UNITED STATES, FOR I DID PROPOSE AT THE UNITED CONFERENCE OF NATIONS THAT THEY SHOULD UNITE ALL OF THE ALLIED SOVEREIGNTIES OF THE WORLD AND LET THERE BE ONE BIG UNITED SOVEREIGNTY. NOW I PROPOSE THE UNIFICATION OF AUSTRALIA, AND NEW ZEALAND, TO THE UNITED STATES, FOR THEY DESIRE TO UNITE WITH THE UNITED STATES OF AMERICA AND BE ONE OF THE STATES OF THE UNION, AND LET US ALL HAVE ONE LANGUAGE AND ONE SPEECH. FOR IT IS WRITTEN:

"And the LORD said, Behold the people is one, and they have all one language; and this they begin to do: and now nothing will be restrained from them, which they have imagined to do!" Genesis 11:6

s/ REV. M. J. DIVINE, Ms.D., D.D.
(Better known as FATHER DIVINE)

REV.MJD:l

(Letter also to President Harry S. Truman)

152

REQUEST FOR SURRENDER OF JAPAN

Rev. M. J. Divine
764-772 S. Broad Street
Philadelphia 46, PA

May 7, 1945 A.D.F.D.

Premier Hirohito
Commander in Chief of the
    Army and Navy of Japan

Your Excellency:

I, Rev. M. J. Divine, known throughout the universe as FATHER DIVINE, for humanity's sake and the redemption of millions of human bodies, do hereby request, appeal and demand of you and yours an immediate unconditional surrender, as you can see the results of this inhuman global war, which has cost the lives of upward of forty million souls. You can see the predicament of your Axis comrades and the destruction they brought upon themselves and their subjects and millions of the American allies, as well as billions of dollars in natural and national resources, only to be obliged to unconditionally surrender or be totally annihilated and become extinct. It is, therefore, essential for you, and the only hope of your redemption and the redemption of your nation, to make an unconditional surrender immediately!

With the hope that others might be even as I AM, this leaves ME Well, Healthy, Joyful, Peaceful, Lively, Loving, Successful, Prosperous and Happy in Spirit, Body and Mind and in every muscle, organ, sinew, joint, limb, vein and bone, and even in every atom, fibre and cell of My Bodily Form.

Respectfully and Sincere, I AM

s/ REV. M. J. DIVINE
(Better known as FATHER DIVINE)

V • • • —— MAIL

CHAPTER 14

THE RIGHTEOUS GOVERNMENT PLATFORM

OF

FATHER DIVINE'S PEACE MISSION MOVEMENT

As Adopted by the
INTERNATIONAL RIGHTEOUS
GOVERNMENT CONVENTION
Held in New York City
January 10th, 11th and 12th, 1936 A.D.F.D.

Editor's Note: Many of the measures which the following document advocates have already been incorporated into city, state and federal government. It is also to be noted that the prices mentioned in the document are those which prevailed during the depression years of the thirties. They of course do not apply to present day Peace Mission prices.

PREAMBLE

PEACE TO ALL! We, the interracial, international, inter-religious, interdenominational and non-partisan co-workers of FATHER DIVINE'S Peace Mission and its Department of Righteous Government, greet all mankind with PEACE! In the light of this New Day and Dispensation in which we are now living since the advent of FATHER DIVINE—Whom twenty-two million have recognized as their Saviour come to earth again in Bodily

Form—we are advocating Righteousness, Justice and Truth in every walk of life. Therefore, we request the cooperation of all governments in legalizing these qualities, and the participation of all right-thinking people in universalizing a Righteous Government.

For this cause, we are assembled in a great International Righteous Government Convention in New York City these three days, the tenth, eleventh and twelfth of January, 1936 A.D.F.D., with Delegates from many different countries and states. The Righteous Government Department of FATHER DIVINE'S Peace Mission Movement has adopted a Platform embodying some of the more important issues of its Righteous Stand. This Platform, which has been verified and endorsed by FATHER DIVINE, with HIS Personal signature, we are privileged to present to you as follows:

In presenting Righteous Government to the world at large, nothing more fitting or far-reaching could be said than what has already been said by HIM Who is the Founder of it, Who has already introduced it to every field of life by establishing it in the lives of twenty-two million followers living in practically every civilized country on earth. A few of HIS Personal Words on the subject, as HE addressed thousands of HIS followers recently in New York City, were as follows:

"It has been through the ages, that religion and the religious teaching have caused men to be submissive, meek and obedient if they were religious, but obedient to wickedness, obedient to dishonesty, obedient to unrighteousness. Therefore, it profited you nothing to be religious and obedient. What profit would it be to us today to bring you into the Spirit and the action of Righteousness, unless we have a Righteous Government? That is why there are so many of the different individuals that have resorted to violence, and refused to accept of the teaching of religion.

"They have striven to keep the CHRIST from the political world. Through the different religions you have been taught that religion and politics will not mix, but I AM privileged to say, without the true concept of CHRIST and the recognition of HIS Presence among the politicians, the world will continue to be filled with corruption, and it is a matter of impossibility to receive your deliverance saving through this great Conversion.

"Righteousness, Truth and Justice shall become to be a living reality, and shall be established universally through legality, and every nation, language, tongue and people shall accept it as the Fundamental."

We believe in these words because we are among the millions that have already been impregnated with these qualities by FATHER DIVINE. Through the New Dispensation of GOD on earth in Bodily Form, we already have a Righteous Government, for Righteousness, Justice and Truth are now reigning in us where unrighteousness, injustice, and untruth once held sway. Therefore we set forth some of the Principles of Righteous Government already established in our midst, and some of the issues involved, that they may be legalized universally.

PRINCIPLES SECTION

That the whole human race is essentially one, and "of one blood GOD formed all nations," has been attested both by Scripture and by science. The Righteous Government of FATHER DIVINE'S Peace Mission stands for and actually produces such an organization of society. It is founded upon the recognition of the Brotherhood of Man and the Fatherhood of GOD. Its Watchword is "Peace," and it actually establishes Peace among the nations by eradicating prejudice, segregation and division from among the people and promoting the welfare of every living creature. From this angle we emphatically protest against the persecution of the Jews in Germany and all other countries, and the oppression of all minorities.

157

This Movement stands for and demands an equal opportunity for every individual without regard to race, creed or color, in accordance with the declaration made in the Constitution of the United States, that all men are created equal. It stands for the Life and Teaching of JESUS THE CHRIST exactly as HE lived it.

We realize that the division of society into political nations has led through the ages to continuous warfare and widespread poverty and distress. Therefore we do not identify ourselves with any nation or people, but we do endorse and support the Constitution of the United States as the Foundation for all governments to build upon. Under the Constitution of the United States, all men can worship GOD according to the dictates of their own conscience, and are guaranteed the right to individual liberty. This has been indicated by FATHER DIVINE as a Divinely established Order for the coming of the Kingdom of GOD on earth.

On every hand however, tendencies can be seen that are undermining the individual liberty and equal rights guaranteed by the Constitution. They are creeping in behind prejudicial and discriminatory laws and ordinances; through the New Deal legislation, and through such laws that deprive the individual of the right to sell his goods for little or nothing if he chooses; through the compulsory insurance laws; the intimidation of workers by the labor unions; the laws imposing compulsory medical treatment, and the like. Concerning the preservation of the Constitution from these reactionary tendencies, FATHER has recently said:

" There is an issue today observed, that had not been observed so vividly as it is now. . . . Laws and by-laws of practically every kind have arisen through the prejudiced representatives of politics among the politicians, that are actually undermining the Constitution of our great country. Just think of laws that are not according to the Constitution, and brought about under the Constitution, which are in complete violation of the Constitution. If GOD would allow it to continue, they would eventually undermine the Constitution completely, and the government of our civilization would be a failure."

INSURANCE IS AGAINST RELIGIOUS BELIEFS

On these issues we stand uncompromisingly for the rights of the common people, and FATHER'S Activities continue silently and unceasingly to eradicate such autocracy. Much of it has already been eliminated. HE is speaking continually in deeds and in actions more than in words, but at various times HE vividly stresses these issues to the masses in words. Concerning the compulsory insurance issue, HE has spoken emphatically. When one of HIS followers and her bondsman, operating a small industry, asked FATHER the question, "Must we take out compensation insurance—as four of us in the shop will have to sign up as partners? If we do not, they will not give us licenses," FATHER replied:

"We will have what we want to have just the same, if we have to get it just the same as the bootleggers and moonshiners do. If they do not give us the right to do what is right without compensation insurances, we will break the law. If they do not allow us to have licenses by the law without taking out insurances, we will run our industries without the law; we will break the law and do it anyhow without any licenses—they just as well to know we will not take out any insurance compensations.

"It is not justifiable to try to force someone against their religious belief, and our religious belief is that we should not take out insurances, and we will not do it. We are willing to get licenses as required by law for anything that is necessary to have licenses for, in a legal way, for the maintenance of the city government, but in regard to insurance compensations and such as that, we will not tolerate it, for it causes men to mistrust GOD, and is not according to our Teaching, and is in violation of our religious belief.

" For this cause we take a stand in opposition to such, but we will get licenses if they choose to give us licenses according to the regulation of the law . . . for the maintenance of the city government and up-keep of the other necessities — official duties, etcetera, for the city — but not insurances to mistrust GOD and visualize disappointments, failures, accidents and disasters. As far as taking out insurances, we will not tolerate it, and I would tell the President so."

COMPULSORY MEDICAL TREATMENT TYRANNICAL

On another occasion, when the question of compulsory medical treatment was brought to an open issue by the authorities, FATHER addressed HIS audience thus:

"According to the law of our state in which we are now living, it is a misdemeanor for a mother or a parent of children under the age of sixteen, not to have a physician, when the cases have been diagnosed as essential for a physical examination and for a physical operation. But I put forth a commandment as for a legal proceeding, to go in the statute books parallel with that which for parents sets up their obligation and a penalty for not having a physician.

"If for any cause MY Spirit and MY Mind, and MY Impersonal Presence, cannot reach your afflicted or sick children or those that are concerned and heal them, you can have a physician and should have one. But remember, the physicians must guarantee the cure and guarantee the life and health of the individual. . . . This is a law within a law and I put it forth as a rebuttal to that of medical science. If they will try to bind mankind in their ruling, they must be subject to a ruling also.

"The physicians and doctors must guarantee a cure, and a complete cure, and the lives of the individuals. If not, they will be held responsible, and sued for the death of the person or persons. Remember, this is Righteousness and Justice and Truth, and we must have it. If we cannot get justice on the side of the common people, we will not give it to the officials. The law is not worth a dime, that is not giving equal rights on either side. The movement is right, but there is another side to it that has been overlooked, and I AM here for the common people. For the masses collectively and universally, I stand.

"Thousands of people are homeless, thousands of them are motherless and fatherless, yea, even familyless. It is indeed Wonderful! Whole families have died by operations. Whole families have been forced to have physicians and still they died, after the physicians and hospitals had taken all their money. It is indeed Wonderful!

"When the physician takes charge of you physically, he must guarantee your health and complete happiness and cure from that affliction and all of the diseases for which they are treating you—if GOD will permit. This is not confined nor bound to this state alone, but any state or country that makes it punishable by law for a person not to have a physician. Hence, this amendment I request for the statute books, as applicable to any person or persons that would be so involved, and to all that are concerned, wheresoever such laws are enacted."

We are unalterably opposed to such unjust laws and such infringements on the rights of the common people, and we ask all legislators and all right-thinking people to cooperate with us in breaking them down.

UNIONS ARE OPPRESSIVE AND UNJUST

But there is a far more important issue by which the rights of millions are being undermined. We refer to the oppression and intimidation of workers by the labor unions. This we will not

161

tolerate. The unjust and autocratic rule these officials and organizations have usurped over the masses, must cease.

Extracting hard-earned money from the workers in the form of heavy membership fees and giving them nothing in return; fining them for the slightest violation of union rules; attempting to regulate the personal affairs of individuals on the jobs; limiting union workers to so many hours a day and five days a week, yet giving them no assurance in return of even that amount of work—such outrages must cease. A rule that does not work both ways cannot be endorsed. Righteousness, Truth and Justice must be observed by all. Speaking to thousands of HIS followers in New York City on this subject, FATHER DIVINE said Personally:

" At this juncture I further wish to convey a thought to the public at large, for which I may have an occasion to call together about fifty thousand for the purpose of universally establishing same, and that is this: Practically all of the different unions, they think they have dominion over the people, and force them to work or force them not to work, and yet give them nothing. I have risen to put it down.

" Every union in the United States of America must deal justly among the people, or else I will strike on them! Just as they have been striking, I will call the laborers together to strike on the unions. It is indeed Wonderful! If you belong to a union, the unions must have a law to see that you get so much work, if you must pay your union dues. If they cannot and will not guarantee you five days' work a week, why then you should withdraw from the unions. It is indeed Wonderful! That is the mystery—that is, if you desire to have the victory!

" Why should the unions try to control the people and put them in slavery? They must deal justly, and it may undoubtedly be a battle on hand. In the places where they work in different factories, talking about the unions coming in and snatching men and women up from their work, when they are working,

getting an honest living! It is Wonderful! I will call a strike on
the unions, if they will not deal justly. That is what I will do! I
will call a strike on the unions! They have oppressed the widow
and the orphan and the hireling in his wages long enough. It is
indeed Wonderful! Going under the name of unions, and will
not guarantee work for the people.

COUNTRY BELONGS TO GOD — NOT TO UNIONS

" Every union that tries to bind the people and put them back
in slavery and prohibit them from working when they are trying
to get an honest living, if they do not pay their dues, how dare
they put their hands on an individual! Now tell them I said keep
their hands off! This country does not belong to the unions, it
belongs to GOD. It is indeed Wonderful! The very idea, talking
about going into men's shops where they have paid for, and
paid taxes in this city, and pulling men and women out of the
jobs. I will put a stop to it! Now tell them I said it, and I
mean it!

" Who are they that you should pay money to anyway? What
have they to do with it? . . . Talking about a man cannot work
unless he belongs to a union, and then joining the union, and
they will not give him work to do! If the union does not
guarantee five days to the week work, according to their
regulations, according to other workers' five day week, why I
will withdraw you all from the unions. I mean what I AM
talking about! . . .

" We are going to have work! We are going to have work with
or without the unions, and if the unions interfere, we will
withdraw from the unions and we are going to work anyhow!
That is what we are going to do! I hope there are some
representing every union under the sound of MY Voice—every
union in the United States of America; I want them all
to hear it.

THE PEACE
MISSION MOVEMENT

"If the labor unions that limit workers to five days a week will guarantee the workers five days' work each week, and will guarantee to pay them what they are demanding from the employers when they call them out on strike, we will endorse them. Otherwise, we will not tolerate them."

In the cause of Righteousness, Justice and Truth, we demand that such infringements on the Constitutional rights of the people be eliminated. We request the lawmakers to make laws and provide machinery to enforce the laws, to safeguard the rights of the common people, and we ask all law-abiding and right-thinking persons to cooperate in observing all righteous and just laws.

We do not mean to say that men can be made righteous, just and truthful by law, for "It is not by power nor by might, but by my spirit, says the LORD." It was not the law that caused millions of people to return stolen goods, to pay up old bills, to become honest, competent and true and be law-abiding citizens when they were just the opposite before they knew FATHER DIVINE; it was HIS Spirit and Mind entering into them. However, the time is at hand for Righteousness, Justice and Truth to be legalized and for those that are unrighteous, unjust and untrue and will not observe the righteousness of the law, to be designated as criminals. Therefore, we demand the following:

Planks For Principles Section

1. Immediate repeal of all laws, ordinances, rules and regulations, local and national, in the United States and elsewhere that have been passed contrary to the spirit and meaning of the Constitution of the United States and its Amendments.

2. Immediate legislation in every state in the Union, and all other states and countries, making it a crime to discriminate in any public place against any individual on account of race, creed or color; abolishing all segregated neighborhoods in cities and towns, making it a crime for landlords or hotels to refuse tenants on such grounds; abolishing all segregated schools and colleges, and all segregated areas in churches, theatres, public conveyances, and other public places.

3. Immediate destruction by both nations and individuals of all firearms and instruments of war within their borders, saving those that are used for law enforcement. (The true followers of FATHER DIVINE will refuse to fight their fellowman for any cause whatsoever.)

4. Legislation making it a crime for any newspaper, magazine, or other publication to use segregated or slang words referring to race, creed or color of any individual or group, or write abusively concerning any.

5. Repeal of all laws or ordinances providing for compulsory insurance, employers' liability, public liability, or any other form of compulsory insurance.

6. Abolishment of capital punishment in all states and countries.

7. Legislation in every state and country where laws or ordinances now exist requiring children or adults to submit to vaccination, operations or treatment by physicians — the new legislation to impose equally binding obligations upon the medical authorities and the physicians. From the moment the authorities or physicians take charge of the patient physically, they must guarantee a complete cure, and guarantee the life of the individual, or be liable for damages in the event of his death.

165

8. Legislation to abolish lynching and outlaw members of lynch mobs in all states and countries.

9. Legislation making it a violation of the law to withhold any kind or classification of work from any civil service employee on account of race, creed or color, provided he or she is qualified to do such work.

10. Immediate return to owners of all stolen goods or their equivalent, not only by individuals but by nations; this to include all territories taken by force from other nations.

11. Legislation making it a crime for any employer to discharge an employee, even though a subordinate, when even circumstantial evidence can be introduced to show that it was on account of race, creed or color.

12. Legislation establishing a maximum fee for all labor union memberships, causing them to accept all qualified applicants, and give them equal privileges regardless of race, creed, color or classification; also providing that any labor union which limits the hours and days of work per week, must guarantee at least that much work per week to its members, and if it calls a strike, pay its members while they are out of work, the full amount they are demanding from the employers; otherwise all obligations for dues must cease.

13. Immediate repeal of all laws and ordinances, governmental rules and regulations requiring individuals to designate themselves as being of a race, creed or color in signing any kind of papers; this to apply especially to immigration, citizenship, passport or legal papers.

14. Legislation making it unlawful for employers of skilled or unskilled, technical or professional help, to have different wage scales or salaries for what they term different races, creeds or colors, or to discriminate in any way in the hiring of help.

ECONOMIC SECTION

The Righteous Government Department of FATHER DIVINE'S Peace Mission bases its plan for universalizing prosperity upon the Fundamental Principle Personified in FATHER DIVINE, that has made millions prosperous. It has taken HIS followers off the relief and made them independent, thus saving the government millions. Not one of HIS true followers would accept of relief in any form, or even so much as go on the relief rolls in order to get a job. We demand the abandonment of the government regulation requiring the people of America to declare themselves destitute and go on the relief rolls in order to get jobs.

The Divine Plan calls for equal distribution of opportunity, and giving every man a chance to be independent—but not so much charity. In the experience of millions who have accepted FATHER DIVINE, all economic and unemployment problems have been solved, and they are actually enjoying the ideal conditions others are striving for. HE has made it possible for those who are cooperative and meek, especially in this country, to live well on five dollars a week or less. HE has further supplied them with part-time jobs at least, to earn an independent living, while causing them to desire to serve their fellowmen in all their waking hours.

A CHANCE TO BE INDEPENDENT

Speaking of HIS Personal Activities in New York, FATHER said:

" I have been feeding the unemployed in a number around about from two thousand five hundred to three thousand a day, but this is not MY great aim in life. This is not the greatest expression. The great expression according to MY version, is to help you to be independent. I will cut out so much feeding of the unemployed as I have been. I have opened ways and means whereby you can get jobs, whereby you can be independent, self-supporting and self-respecting. That is what I AM desiring to see you all do and be.

167

" Therefore I have made the way possible for the last three years or more, in the City of New York and elsewhere, that you might be able to get by at from four to five dollars a week and be independent. If you come here, or go any place and get a meal for ten or fifteen cents, you do not have to feel as a beggar.

" You can feel independent, for that is the price, or those are the prices for the meals in all of our Connections, not only here in New York City, but all the way across the country in all of the places—fifteen cents is the maximum fee for a meal. I wish to further announce . . . hereafter our barber shops will not charge but ten cents for a haircut for men, and five cents for a shave . . . . We shall make simular cuts in the dress shops in proportion, and in the grocery stores, and other expressions of our industries."

Naturally the cost of these facilities is greater than the income from them, and no man could continue indefinitely to carry them on, but as they are the gift of GOD to mankind, they are amply provided for. FATHER DIVINE takes no collections, accepts no donations or financial support whatsoever, and has never been known to do so. On the contrary, HE is constantly giving.

FREE EMPLOYMENT BUREAU

Another of HIS Personal Activities for the benefit of the masses has been a free employment agency. After operating HIS own private agency free for many years, HE recently opened up a public agency to get at the intolerable conditions in the employment field. Regarding these conditions, HE recently spoke as follows:

" I call your attention to an incident just happening now here in your midst which I AM in, and that is this: I took over and opened up the Busy Bee Employment Agency. The law has been for years that the employees and the employers are supposed to pay ten percent to the agency . . . but I learned since I have been in it, that the employers will not pay a penny. They have been forcing the employees to pay their ten percent and the employers not paying anything. It is indeed Wonderful! But I will not have it that way longer.

"That is one of the outrages that has been manifested or concealed here . . . where they would force the employees to pay their fees, but would not force the employers, who have millions, to pay a fee. Many of the employees did not have bread to eat, neither a place to sleep, seeking work to be honest, competent and true, and yet if they got a chance to get a position, they could not have it unless they paid their fees; yet the millionaire that was hiring them as the employer—they would not charge him a penny. It is indeed Wonderful!

"In every little simple expression, you can see the outward expression of the oppression of those who are as the hireling and the fatherless, the poor and the needy, the laboring class of people. It is indeed Wonderful! As I said some time ago, . . . I will get you positions if you are competent. If you have good references, I will get you positions, free of charge. I will let you go free—the employee—but the employers can pay their fee."

Planks For Economic Section

1. Legislation prohibiting employment agencies from collecting fees or remuneration in any form from employees, but authorizing them to collect the present legal fees in full from the employers; also the establishment of a minimum wage scale, prohibiting agencies from sending out workers for less than their respective minimum rates.

2. Government control of all idle plants and machinery, tools and equipment, where owners are unwilling to

operate them at full capacity; such facilities to be made available to workers on a cooperative, non-profit basis under supervision of government experts, with temporary provision for materials; workers to be paid a living wage until income exceeds expenses; then the wage scale to be increased and maintained at as high a rate as conditions permit. The owners would have the privilege of operating the plants at any time they are willing and able to operate them at full capacity, until some arrangement is made for change of ownership.

3.   Immediate abandonment of the government regulation requiring individuals to be on the relief rolls in order to get work on relief projects.

4.   Immediate provision, under government supervision, of work on useful projects, for every unemployed worker according to his qualifications, with suitable pay for amount of work accomplished. (Expenditures for many such projects, such as high speed tunnels, express highways, or whatsoever it might be, could quickly be regained by tolls, as in the case of the Holland Tunnel in New York City.)

5.   Immediate abondonment by all states and countries, of government crop control, destruction of food stuffs and other products, and the establishment of an efficient and equitable distribution system. (The spectacle of hungry people in a land of plenty is worse than uncivilized.)

6.   Laws to be altered so that equal opportunity is allowed to all, that every worker be allowed access to the land, to the tools and materials needed for the carrying out of his individual talent, for the welfare of himself and of society.

7.   Abolition of all tariff schedules and obstacles to free trade among the nations. Trade among all the peoples of

the earth should be left as free as is now the trade among the various states of the American Union.

8. Legislation limiting the amount of profit to be made on any article or product, but leaving the individual free to sell it for as little as he chooses.

9. Government to print its own money, and make it illegal to hoard it. Government to redeem all its bonded debts and to lend the money to the cooperative non-profit enterprises; abolish all interest and make it a criminal offense to take usury or interest, or to receive dividends that exceed 3½ percent, or money without labor performed or practical service rendered.

10. Government ownership and operation of the financial system.

11. Legislation making it a criminal offense for any individual to spend money except for necessities of life, while he owes a just debt to any other individual or organization. (The followers of FATHER DIVINE will not owe another, and will not buy on the installment plan.)

12. Immediate destruction of all counterfeit money by those who have acquired it, rather than attempting to pass it on; and a change in the currency to eliminate all counterfeits in circulation. (The followers of FATHER DIVINE destroy all counterfeit money they find in circulation, at their own expense, rather than pass it on to another.)

FATHER said in a recent message:

"Now in reference to counterfeit money; whensoever one has a counterfeit dollar, a counterfeit fifty-dollar bill, or counterfeit of any denomination of a bill or money, it matters not what it is, if it would be a thousand dollars, if you find out that it is counterfeit, this counterfeit expression should be destroyed. If someone else happens to pass a counterfeit dollar on you, destroy it immediately. If you find that it is a counterfeit dollar, and you are convinced that it is counterfeit, you should destroy it, for it is false; therefore, you should destroy the false."

It is not claimed that the recommendations contained in this Platform will solve every economic problem of the world at large, but the Fundamental Principle will. In FATHER DIVINE is found the solution of every problem that may arise. Neither is it claimed that legislation alone can solve the problem, but as we have already stated, Righteousness, Justice and Truth must be legalized, and all unrighteousness, injustice and untruth outlawed.

The Principles advocated are just a few of those that FATHER DIVINE has established in the lives of millions. They have changed underworld characters into upright citizens. They have changed dishonesty and good-for-nothingness into honesty, competence and truth; making millions prosperous and independent of relief, causing them to return stolen goods and pay old bills they never intended to pay. Thus, FATHER has saved the government, public utilities, companies, department stores, and business as a whole, millions of dollars annually, and caused millions to seek justice through Righteousness, when they might have sought it in unrighteousness, through force of arms.

POLITICAL SECTION

Speaking of politics and politicians and HIS participation with them, FATHER has said:

"They have striven to keep the CHRIST completely out of politics, telling you GOD and religious people would not be in politics in the corruptibleness of the politicians and the wickedness of the wicked; HE would not function in their expression—but HE came among them to convert them. For this cause I AM and have as much right in politics as I have in the church, and really, I have more right in politics than I have in the church. As politics elects officials to rule the people, GOD must be in it, as GOD must rule them. If GOD does not rule them, you are ruined.

"Righteousness, Justice and Truth among the politicians must be legalized. Non-partisanism is the great expression through which GOD can express. Even though you be of a special party, as I said the other evening, your only hope of expressing Truth, Righteousness and Justice, is to have non-partisan ideas and opinions—the same as a family. You may be of one family but you are not qualified to be an official elected by the people to serve the people unselfishly unless you leave that idea of your immediate family and serve all humanity."

The followers of FATHER DIVINE belong to no one party or organization, though they may cooperate with many, under FATHER'S Leading, in the cause of Righteousness, Justice and Truth. They vote for the candidate who is best fitted to fill the office, regardless of his political affiliation, if they are convinced that he will deal justly, with Truth and Righteousness. If his public or private life has ever shown prejudice, bigotry or discrimination, vice, crime, or opposition to the reign of CHRIST; if his record shows tendencies of selfishness, graft, greed or political corruption, they don't want him in office regardless of his promises.

A very efficient research department is maintained in the Righteous Government program, to gather this information and record the stand of the officials of our city, state and federal government on the various issues, and this information is available to all.

Through the Righteous Government Department's political activities, FATHER has qualified many thousands to register and vote intelligently, who never had voted and never would have voted otherwise, and many more are being qualified now. Those who needed citizenship papers and had no means to pay for them, FATHER has paid the fees Personally, provided they entered the country legally.

When the lower courts and the Board of Elections of New York refused the new names of the followers, FATHER carried them through the Supreme Court and had them legalized. The Supreme Court reversed the decision of the lower courts and now it is legal to register and vote in any name under which a person is known, regardless of how peculiar it may sound to the officials.

FATHER has caused millions to take a new interest in voting in the cause of Righteous Government, and though HE insists that they follow their own highest intuition as to whom they vote for, they would move as a unit at HIS slightest Command, or upon HIS endorsement of a candidate. Even without HIS Spoken Word, they are unified in the one Spirit and Mind, to vote the right man into office, and the wrong man out. This will be done anyhow, for FATHER'S Mind and Spirit have access in the hearts and minds of the masses.

For the advancement of Righteousness, Justice and Truth in the political world, we request the following:

Planks For Political Section

1. That all candidates, including candidates for president, be nominated entirely by the people, and that they be required to meet specified requirements, to prove their qualifications for office, not as politicians, but technical experts.
2. Immediate abandonment of the political patronage system and appointment of all Civil Service employees strictly according to their qualifications and service, and their standing on the list, without regard to party, race, creed or color, and without the intervention of political leaders.

BIGOTED OFFICIALS

Following FATHER'S Example, others of FATHER'S Movement endeavored to open licensed employment agencies and cooperate in the same work of helping the masses, but the commissioners showed every evidence of a desire to uphold and perpetrate the old system of squeezing small sums out of the poor and letting the employers go free, and they would not grant licenses. FATHER spoke in this regard as follows:

"It has been distinctly understood that wheresoever there is an application put in for an employment agency, the prejudicial officials in connection with the administration are trying to keep MY co-workers or anyone who is connected with ME, from having an employment agency. It is because they know within themselves, I will cut the cost of living.

"They know I AM here as a help for the meek and lowly. They know that I came as a swift witness against those who will oppress the widow and the fatherless, and will not come nigh ME. That is why they are trying to keep MY Connection out of it.

"I will put it through if I have to put them out of office! That is what I will do! Everyone who comes in opposition, everyone who will rise in an endeavor to oppose MY Endeavors, I shall put them to an open shame. Every prejudicial official who is in the commission, and connected in any way in this administration, who desires to prohibit ME from having an employment agency Personally, I shall put him out of office. There are thousands of people out of work, without food and shelter and I can see the oppressed—the widows and the orphans, the hireling in his wages—and I will bring swift judgment to the offender."

175

EQUAL OPPORTUNITY FOR ALL

Unlike other plans—that have been declared economically un-
sound and impractical on account of the tremendous expenditures
involved—the Divine Plan requires nothing that is not already
available. It is based on cooperation, equal opportunity, and the
recognition of the Brotherhood of Man and the Fatherhood of
GOD. Wealth, if it is to continue to exist and prosper in this New
Day, must be continually used for the benefit of humanity, and not
for selfish gains.

If all idle plants and machinery, and available lands now
costing billions in taxes and upkeep, were immediately made
available to the workers, they would soon become profitable, and
the eleven millions now said to be unemployed in the United
States would soon be employed. The Divine Plan means work, and
more work, with prices of commodities reduced to a minimum.

As a sample and an example of how wealth should be used,
FATHER is buying large tracts of land in one of the best parts of
the State of New York and making homesites available to the peo-
ple free. Speaking along this line at HIS Righteous Government
Forum in New York City recently, FATHER spoke the following
Words to the masses assembled:

" The earth is the LORD'S and the fullness thereof, but yet HE
does not claim everything Personally. . . . At the Day of
Pentecost, they had all things in common, did they not?

"I AM not asking you all to buy, neither to help ME buy a
piece of property. I have purchased the property—several
places—and they are all free and clear. . . . If perchance you
have the means, or will have the means to build a home, the
ground, the land, the lots will be given to you free of cost, and
you will have your deeds for them without a string tied to them.
This is an abstract expression of the idea of making all things
common, claiming nothing for yourself as an individual, refus-

ing to hoard up riches for yourselves for a selfish purpose, but give everybody a chance to enjoy some of it."

The followers of FATHER DIVINE in every community, state, province, colony and nation, have the opportunity of becoming an example for all governments, by cooperative living and a universal pooling of all of their interests. They can become an independent unit even as these in New York City, according to the example set by FATHER'S Personal Activities. HE has made living accommodations of the best available in the world's most expensive city, for from one to two dollars a week, bountiful meals of high quality for ten and fifteen cents, with dress shops, tailor shops, grocery stores, bus lines, boat excursions, special trains and other facilities available at similarly low prices.

Advocating equal distribution of opportunity, a chance for every man, plenty of work with good wages, prices reduced to a minimum, and all of the advantages for the masses, we are now enjoying these things and we know they can be enjoyed by all. Therefore, we request the following:

EDUCATIONAL SECTION

Through the educational program of the Righteous Government Department, those of the masses who are not already qualified are being qualified to pass the literacy tests, to register and to vote intelligently, to pass Civil Service examinations, and to fill any office they might be called upon to fill. They are attending the evening schools in such numbers, the local schools in the city of New York have not been sufficient to accommodate them and extra facilities have been provided. In the Kingdom and its extensions, private schools have been established under the direction of regular teachers, to care for the needs of those who are otherwise engaged during school hours, and there are many such schools throughout the country.

For the advancement of real education and culture among the
people, we request the following:

Planks For Educational Section

1. The doors of all educational institutions to be open and free
   to all for universal education, with same rights for all to
   higher technical and professional training.
2. The abolishing in all educational institutions, and from
   books used for educational purposes in such institutions, of
   all references to racial conflicts or differences, and national
   glory through military feats, etcetera, with legislation making it a misdemeanor for any educator to teach such to
   his classes.
3. The abolishing of the conventional form of greeting,
   "H-e-l-l-o," from all educational institutions, and substi-
   tution of the word "Peace." We also request the cooperation of the telephone companies in this respect, that a
   generation with Peace on its lips, instead of what war has
   been said to be, may come into being.

In concluding our Educational Platform, we could not do
better than to quote the Words of our Beloved Saviour
FATHER DIVINE, Who has come to us again in this New Dispensation, bringing "Peace on Earth, and Good Will to Men," Whom
we have recognized as the same Identical CHRIST with all Power
and Dominion, reigning now and forevermore as the Everlasting
FATHER and the Prince of Peace in Bodily Form. HE has said:

" We will get just what we demand from every angle expressible, and we shall get it through legality by the ballot, and not
by the bullet. For this cause I have encouraged and stirred the
nation with the desire and ambition to seek a better education
that you might be qualified to pass the literacy test in whatsoever state you are living; that you might be able to go to the

polls and cast your ballots on the days of election, and vote in that one you are convinced will deal justly, and vote out the unjust official. . . .

"We will use the legal and political guns, but refuse to use those that are the expressers of destruction, for we are not conceivers of destructive ideas and opinions. Therefore we will not resort to violence through destroying mankind nor the visible things that pertain to this life, but we will destroy every endeavor or act of an unrighteous official and put them out of commission, that they might have no longer an existence among the people in unrighteousness and corruption.

"Righteousness, Truth and Justice must become to be a Living Reality, and as I have brought it thus far through legality, it shall be universally established . . . and every nation, language, tongue and people shall accept it as the Fundamental."

We thank YOU, FATHER!

Righteous Government Department
FATHER DIVINE'S Peace Mission Movement

Verified and Endorsed by

s/ REVEREND M. J. DIVINE
Better known as FATHER DIVINE

AMENDMENTS

Planks For Principles Section
Add to Plank Number 8:

8. Legislation imposing the penalty for first degree murder on all members of lynch mobs killing or fatally injuring any person, together with a fine of ten to twenty thousand dollars to be paid by the county wherein the lynching occurs, to the estate of the injured or deceased person.

In bringing forth this amendment and speaking particularly of the Costigan-Wagner Anti-lynching Bill, FATHER said:

" I just wish to say in reference to the Anti-lynching Bill, if this is not inserted in it, it is not severe enough. This of which I AM about to say, was and is—if one person will murder a man without the law, he is subject to punishment to the extent as being termed a murderer. . . . If two men will commit the same crime, many of them have been charged as a murderer and received the penalty of the same. This should be in the Anti-lynching Bill.

"Every man in a lynch mob should be convicted as a murderer—not one alone, but every one—for they are all murderers, and if we would tolerate it, they would continue to indulge in wholesale murder by getting together by the hundreds and by the thousands. Therefore I say, a lynch mob does murder. It is an organization, an organized body of murderers. Every member of a lynch mob that would lynch a man should go to the same place wheresoever men are supposed to go when they commit that crime."

Planks For Educational Section
Add Plank Number 4:

4. The adoption of a universal language by all nations, languages, tongues and peoples—all governments to assist

in establishing it by including it in the courses of study in all public schools and colleges.

Concerning this subject, FATHER has Personally spoken as follows:

" For the purpose of bringing all men together, I came to convert all of the systems. There shall be no division after a while in language. There shall be one language. Now isn't that Wonderful! Firstly it was essential to eradicate and abolish divisons among us as races, creeds and colors supposedly, but for the Perfect Work to be accomplished, there will not even be divisions in systems, languages, tongues nor people, for they all shall understand each other with the one language we are speaking.

" Now I did not say especially, it must be broken English as I AM speaking, but whatsoever language Divine Love and GOD'S Omniscience finds sufficient and quite efficient for the purpose, will be adopted, and all people shall talk it. I AM not especially trying to justify the American language as broken English, neither AM I especially trying to adopt it as the international language, but as a Representative of Righteousness, Truth and Justice, I AM seeking a language to be spoken that will be of more effect, and more suitable for all nations, languages, tongues and people."

We thank YOU, FATHER!

Righteous Government Department
FATHER DIVINE'S Peace Mission Movement

Verified and Endorsed by

s/ REVEREND M. J. DIVINE
Better known as FATHER DIVINE

MOTHER DIVINE accepts a Resolution from the President and members of the Philadelphia City Council February 18, 1982 A.D. 36 F.D.

CHAPTER 15

Philadelphia City Council Commends Peace Mission Movement

COUNCIL OF THE CITY OF PHILADELPHIA
OFFICE OF THE CHIEF CLERK
ROOM 402, CITY HALL
PHILADELPHIA

(Resolution No. 689)

RESOLUTION

Lauding and commending the Peace Mission Movement for over half a century of dedication and service to God and the community.

WHEREAS, The Peace Mission Movement, founded by The Reverend, Major J. Divine, better known as Father Divine, over 50 years ago, has fought long and hard against discrimination of all types; and

WHEREAS, The world-wide Peace Mission Movement has provided more than 40 years of service to the Philadelphia community through its churches, hotels, cafeterias, food markets, dress shops, barber shops, gas stations, shoe repair and dry cleaning establishments, and such other services that provide the necessities of life, generally at lower prices than can be found elsewhere in the community; and

WHEREAS, The Peace Mission Movement has fed the hungry, clothed and sheltered thousands of people who were destitute, homeless, and in despair, without any charge to the recipients; and

WHEREAS, The followers of Father Divine are dedicated to the Law of Americanism, Brotherhood, and Christianity, and the followers exemplify through their works, words, and deeds high respect for the dignity of every human being; and

WHEREAS, The Peace Mission Movement has been active in encouraging neighborhood children to do well in school by providing afterschool classes and individual tutoring and has provided recreational programs that offer young people constructive alternatives to gangs or other forms of anti-social behavior; and

WHEREAS, The followers of Father Divine are peace loving, work for brotherhood and unity, and are opposed to fighting, war, racism, and violence of all kinds, and the followers eschew personal habits which are destructive to the mental, physical, or emotional health, including all forms of drugs, alcohol, and tobacco, as well as coarse language; the followers greet each other with love and peace, which they wish for all the peoples of the world, which sets an example for individuals, families and nations to emulate; therefore

Resolved by the Council of the City of Philadelphia, That we hereby laud and commend the Peace Mission Movement for over half a century of dedication and service to God and the community.

Further Resolved, That an Engrossed copy of this Resolution be presented to Mother Divine as evidence of the sincere sentiments of this legislative body.

CERTIFICATION: This is a true and correct copy of the original Resolution adopted by the Council of the City of Philadelphia on the fourth day of February, 1982.

s/ Joseph E. Coleman
President of City Council

ATTEST:

s/ Charles H. Sawyer, Jr.
Chief Clerk of the Council

Introduced by

Augusta Clark	David Cohen
Lucien E. Blackwell	John F. Street
John C. Anderson	

Sponsored by

Joseph E. Coleman	Joan L. Krajewski
Augusta A. Clark	Ann Land
John C. Anderson	Brian J. O'Neill
Lucien E. Blackwell	Francis Rafferty
David Cohen	Joan Specter
John F. Street	James J. Tayoun
Harry P. Jannotti	Anna Cibotti Verna

The International Peace card which many people all over the world carry with them at all times as a remembrance of the protective Presence of GOD being constantly with them.

EPILOGUE

It is our pleasure to have explained the fundamental Truths of Life that have shaped the day to day living of the followers of FATHER DIVINE in this wonderful experience of the Peace Mission Movement. This experience has carried us on the spiritual journey that JESUS CHRIST beckoned all the world to take, and about which John Bunyan wrote in his *Pilgrim's Progress.*

We trust that the reader will now better understand those of us who have embraced the Peace Mission Movement. We also hope that this book will contribute to the elevation of the human race as it ascends into the glorious Liberty of the Christ Life.

PEACE

INDEX

INDEX *(continued)*